TEACHER'S PET PUBLICATIONS

LITPLAN TEACHER PACK
for
The Egypt Game
based on the book by
Zilpha Keatley Snyder

Written by
Catherine Caldwell

© 2006 Teacher's Pet Publications
All Rights Reserved

This **LitPlan** for
The Egypt Game
has been brought to you by Teacher's Pet Publications, Inc.

Copyright Teacher's Pet Publications 2006

Only the student materials in this unit plan (such as worksheets, study questions, and tests) may be reproduced multiple times for use in the purchaser's classroom.

For any additional copyright questions,
contact Teacher's Pet Publications.

www.tpet.com

TABLE OF CONTENTS - *The Egypt Game*

Introduction	5
Unit Objectives	7
Reading Assignment Sheet	8
Unit Outline	9
Study Questions (Short Answer)	13
Quiz/Study Questions (Multiple Choice)	28
Pre-reading Vocabulary Worksheets	59
Lesson One (Introductory Lesson)	79
Nonfiction Assignment Sheet	83
Oral Reading Evaluation Form	85
Writing Assignment 1	94
Writing Assignment 2	104
Writing Assignment 3	107
Writing Evaluation Form	95
Vocabulary Review Activities	96
Extra Writing Assignments/Discussion ?s	98
Unit Review Activities	109
Unit Tests	113
Unit Resource Materials	159
Vocabulary Resource Materials	181

A FEW NOTES ABOUT THE AUTHOR
Zilpha Keatley Snyder

"When I look back to the beginning, at least as far back as memory will take me, I see most vividly animals and games and books."
-Zilpha Keatley Snyder

Zilpha Keatley Snyder was born during the Depression of the 1930s and spent her childhood in rural California. Her father, who had spent his own youth on a cattle ranch, established the family in the country where they could have a garden and animals. Though she can remember the hardships that characterized the Depression, including the ever-present threat of unemployment, she recalls more vividly the life she spent with books and her own powerful imagination. She brought the stories she read in literature and the bible to her own room, her own yard, her own world-- re-enacting them in glorious detail. By age four, Snyder was an accomplished reader, devouring anything in print--from children's books to newspapers. Her mother, too, filled the home with stories, most of them true, and Snyder claims to have discovered her future occupation before reaching high school.

Always a strong student, Snyder enrolled at Whittier College, a small liberal arts school in Southern California, after completing high school. It was at Whittier that she met her husband, Larry Snyder, whom she married on June 18, 1950. The couple moved around a great deal during the years of World War II, and they had three children. Although Snyder knew that she wanted to become a writer, she became a teacher of young adults first until she could find the time to devote to writing. During her work with young people, Snyder realized that she was drawn to the wonder of childhood. While she acknowledges that many authors do not consider the age of their audience as they are composing their works, Snyder consciously writes most of her books for children. By writing for young people, she claims, she is able to share the optimism, curiosity, and boundless possibility that characterizes youth.

Her first novel, *Season of Ponies*, was published in 1964, and she has not stopped writing since. The Egypt Game was her fourth novel, published in 1967 by Atheneum books. It received a Newbery Honor, as did *The Headless Cupid* (1971) and *The Witches of Worm* (1972). Mrs. Snyder is the author of over 40 books, and she has received countless awards since she began her career. She has spent much of her time over the past two decades writing novels and traveling the globe with her husband. She looks forward to continuing both for a long time.

INTRODUCTION

This LitPlan has been designed to develop students' reading, writing, thinking, and language skills through exercises and activities related to *The Egypt Game*. It includes 23 lessons, supported by extra resource materials.

The **introductory lesson** introduces students to the process of group collaboration and compromise as students are asked to work with their group members to develop rules for a game that has no established rules. Following the introductory activity, students are given a transition to explain how the activity relates to the book they are about to read. Students also are given the materials they will be using during the unit. The class will also have an opportunity to draw conclusions about the novel based on a cursory examination of the cover and table of contents.

The **reading assignments** are approximately thirty pages each; some are a little shorter while others are a little longer. Students have approximately 15 minutes of pre-reading work to do prior to each reading assignment. This pre-reading work involves reviewing the study questions for the assignment and doing some vocabulary work for 10 to 12 vocabulary words they will encounter in their reading.

The **study guide questions** are fact-based questions; students can find the answers to these questions right in the text. These questions come in two formats: short answer or multiple choice. The best use of these materials is probably to use the short answer version of the questions as study guides for students (since answers will be more complete), and to use the multiple choice version for occasional quizzes.

The **vocabulary work** is intended to enrich students' vocabularies as well as to aid in the students' understanding of the book. Prior to each reading assignment, students will complete a two-part worksheet for approximately 10 to 12 vocabulary words in the upcoming reading assignment. Part I focuses on students' use of general knowledge and contextual clues by giving the sentence in which the word appears in the text. Students are then to write down what they think the words mean based on each word's usage. Part II nails down the definitions of the words by giving students dictionary definitions of the words and having students match the words to the correct definitions based on the words' contextual usage. Students should then have an understanding of the words when they meet them in the text.

After each reading assignment, students will go back and formulate answers for the study guide questions. Discussion of these questions serves as a **review** of the most important events and ideas presented in the reading assignments.

After students complete their reading of the work, there is a **vocabulary review** lesson which pulls together all of the fragmented vocabulary lists for the reading assignments and gives students a review of all of the words they have studied.

Following the vocabulary review, a lesson is devoted to the **extra discussion questions/writing assignments**. These questions focus on interpretation, critical analysis and personal response, employing a variety of thinking skills and adding to the students' understanding of the novel.

There is a **group theme project** in this unit. Students will divide into groups of 5 or 6 students in order to simulate the size of the fictional group of Egyptians in *The Egypt Game*. Each group will research a particular aspect of ancient Egypt presented in the novel. Each group will then develop an original product based on their research. A presentation day is scheduled in the unit so that students may benefit from one another's work, in addition to practicing their public speaking skills.

There are three **writing assignments** in this unit, each with the purpose of informing, persuading, or having students express personal opinions. The first writing assignment asks students to compose a diary entry based on a character's conflict in the novel. The second writing assignment asks the students to write a newspaper article recounting an episode that occurs towards the end of novel. The third writing assignment requires students to choose an aspect about their school they would like to change and formulate a plan for effecting such change.

There is a **nonfiction reading assignment**. Students must read nonfiction articles, books, etc. to gather information about themes in our world today. They will then complete a worksheet pertaining to material they have read.

The **review lesson** pulls together all of the aspects of the unit. The teacher is given four or five choices of activities or games to use which all serve the same basic function of reviewing all of the information presented in the unit.

The **unit test** comes in two formats: multiple choice and short answer. As a convenience, two different tests for each format have been included. There is also an advanced short answer unit test for advanced students.

There are additional **support materials** included with this unit. The **Unit Resource Materials** section includes suggestions for an in-class library, crossword and word search puzzles related to the novel, and extra worksheets. There is a list of **bulletin board ideas** which gives the teacher suggestions for bulletin boards to go along with this unit. In addition, there is a list of **extra class activities** the teacher could choose from to enhance the unit or as a substitution for an exercise the teacher might feel is inappropriate for his/her class. **Answer keys** are located directly after the **reproducible student materials** throughout the unit. The **Vocabulary Resource Materials** section includes similar worksheets and games to reinforce the vocabulary words.

The **level** of this unit can be varied depending upon the criteria on which the individual assignments are graded, the teacher's expectations of his/her students in class discussions, and the formats chosen for the study guides, quizzes and test. If teachers have other ideas/activities they wish to use, they can usually easily be inserted prior to the review lesson.

UNIT OBJECTIVES - *The Egypt Game*

1. Students will demonstrate their understanding of the text on four levels: factual, interpretive, critical and personal.

2. Students will gain a better understanding of ancient Egypt and its influence on the present day.

3. Students will examine some of the various family relationships and dynamics that exist in America.

4. Students will gain a better understanding of internal and external conflicts in *The Egypt Game*.

5. Students will gain experience researching a given topic using a variety of media.

6. Students will be given the opportunity to practice reading aloud and silently to improve their skills in each area.

7. Students will answer questions to demonstrate their knowledge and understanding of the main events and characters in *The Egypt Game* as they relate to the author's theme development.

8. Students will enrich their vocabularies and improve their understanding of the novel through the vocabulary lessons prepared for use in conjunction with the novel.

9. The writing assignments in this unit are geared to several purposes:
    a. To have students demonstrate their abilities to inform, to persuade, or to express their own personal ideas
       Note: Students will demonstrate ability to write effectively to <u>inform</u> by developing and organizing facts to convey information. Students will demonstrate the ability to write effectively to <u>persuade</u> by selecting and organizing relevant information, establishing an argumentative purpose, and by designing an appropriate strategy for an identified audience. Students will demonstrate the ability to write effectively to <u>express personal ideas</u> by selecting a form and its appropriate elements.
    b. To check the students' reading comprehension
    c. To make students think about the ideas presented by the novel
    d. To encourage logical thinking
    e. To provide an opportunity to practice good grammar and improve students' use of the English language

10. Students will examine the author's use of diction and imagery in the novel.

READING ASSIGNMENT SHEET - *The Egypt Game*

Date Assigned	Chapters Assigned	Completion Date
	Chapters 1-2	
	Chapters 3-4	
	Chapters 5-6	
	Chapters 7-9	
	Chapters 10-12	
	Chapters 13-15	
	Chapters 16-19	
	Chapters 20-23	

UNIT OUTLINE - *The Egypt Game*

1 Introduction	2 PV 1-2 Read Ch 1-2	3 PV 3-4 Read Ch 3-4 HW: SGQ	4 PV Ch 5-6 Read Ch 5-6 HW:SGQ	5 PV Ch 7-9 Read Ch 7-9 HW: SGQ
6 Quiz Ch 1-9 PV Ch 10-12 Read Ch 10-12 HW: SGQ	7 Group: SGQ: Ch 10-12 PV 13-15 HW: Read Ch 13-15	8 Group: SGQ:Ch 13-15 PV 16-19 HW: Read 16-19	9 PV 20-23 Read 20-23	10 Group assignments
11 Writing Assignment 1	12 Vocabulary	13 Library Day and Writing conferences	14 Extra Discussion Questions	15 Nonfiction: Reports
16 Journalism Study	17 Writing Assignment 2	18 Creating a Mood	19 Writing Assignment 3	20 Egypt Group Presentations
21 Playing our Egypt Game: What was it like?	22 Review	23 Test	24	25

Key: P = Preview Study Questions   V = Vocabulary Work   R= Read
SGQ = Study Guide Questions

STUDY GUIDE QUESTIONS

SHORT ANSWER STUDY GUIDE QUESTIONS - *The Egypt Game*

Chapter 1: "The Discovery of Egypt"
1. Who owns the curio store?
2. Where is the store located?
3. How do people in the community generally feel about the Professor?
4. Who first witnesses the Egypt Game?
5. What are the names of the three children the Professor watches through the window?
6. What is Marshall carrying with him?

Chapter 2: "Enter April"
1. What does April Hall sometimes call herself?
2. What is the name of the building where April comes to live?
3. Who is Dorothea?
4. Who is Caroline?
5. What happened to April's father?
6. Where does Caroline work?
7. Who is April supposed to "check in" with before leaving the building?
8. What does April purchase from the drug store?
9. Why is April impressed by the man at A-Z?
10. What does April tell the man she wants to be when she grows up?

Chapter 3: "Enter Melanie–and Marshall"
1. Why is Melanie hopeful as she knocks on Apartment 312?
2. What is Melanie's initial reaction when April opens the door?
3. Why doesn't April think Melanie will like her?
4. How does April first describe her mother's job to Melanie?
5. What does April learn about Mrs. Ross from her smile?
6. What is Melanie's "favorite occupation?"
7. What makes April finally take off her eyelashes?
8. What does Melanie keep hidden in the "dull-looking old geography book?"
9. How does April react to Melanie's secret hobby?
10. What name does Melanie give to the games that the girls play?

Chapter 4: "The Egypt Girls"
1. Where do Melanie and April go almost everyday in August?
2. How do April and Melanie earn the name "the Egypt girls?"
3. Why are April and Melanie worried about the start of school?
4. What aspect of April's appearance most concerns Melanie?
5. What reason does April give Melanie for her feelings about Caroline?
6. What do April, Marshall, and Melanie find in the deserted yard that April considers "a beautiful messenger from out of the ancient past?"

Egypt Game Study Questions Page 2

Chapter 5: "The Evil God and the Secret Spy"
  1. Who does Melanie suggest might be watching them through the window?
  2. Who do the girls appoint pharaoh?
  3. What do they name the pharaoh?
  4. Why does Marshall agree to play the game?
  5. Who is Set?
  6. Where do the girls get the rules for the Egypt game?
  7. What happens–unbeknownst to the girls–after they throw the boxes over the fence?

Chapter 6: "Eyelashes and Ceremony"
  1. Why is April having trouble concentrating the day before school is to begin?
  2. Why is Melanie having trouble concentrating?
  3. What does Melanie take from April's room? How?
  4. How do the sixth graders at Wilson respond to April?
  5. What nickname do Toby and Ken give to April? Why is it important?
  6. What do Isis and Nefertiti represent?
  7. How are the rituals of the Egypt game recorded?
  8. What is the Crocodile Stone? What do the girls do with it?
  9. Why does Mr. Ross believe that Marshall depends on Security?

Chapter 7: "Neferbeth"
  1. Who moves into Casa Rosada in September? How old is she?
  2. What subjects is Mr. Ross preparing to teach?
  3. Who does Elizabeth look like to April and Melanie?
  4. Why do April and Melanie ask Elizabeth to join the Egypt game?

Chapter 8: "Prisoners of Fear"
  1. How does Elizabeth respond to the Egypt Game?
  2. What name do Melanie and April give to Elizabeth in the game?
  3. What puts a temporary stop to the Egypt game?
  4. Who does the community begin to believe is guilty?
  5. Who organizes the efforts to invite the Professor to leave?
  6. How do the players continue the Egypt game when they are confined to the Casa Rosada?
  7. How do accusations against the Professor affect his business?
  8. What weighs on April's mind when she doesn't have the Egypt Game to occupy her time?
  9. What changes do the players notice in Egypt when they stop by briefly?

Egypt Game Study Questions Page 3

Chapter 9: "Summoned by the Mighty Ones"
   1. Under what circumstances are the kids in the neighborhood allowed to trick-or-treat?
   2. What is April's plan for revisiting Egypt?
   3. What costumes do April, Elizabeth, Melanie, and Marshall wear for Halloween?
   4. What token does April claim Set and Isis have sent to the players as a summons?
   5. What are the players watching for as they trick-or-treat?

Chapter 10: "The Return to Egypt"
   1. Why does Marshall ask to hold a sign as he is standing with the other trick-or-treaters?
   2. Who do the girls run into while trick-or-treating?
   3. Describe Toby's and Ken's costumes.
   4. What does the Egypt gang claim to be the secret omen?

Chapter 11: "Egypt Invaded"
   1. What does April declare the Crocodile God demands for sacrifice?
   2. What does Marshall mumble under his breath after April tells him not to yell?
   3. What do the players decide to use for sacrifice?
   4. What happens at the end of the Ceremony of Sacrifice?

Chapter 12: "Elizabethan Diplomacy"
   1. Who enters Egypt uninvited?
   2. Why does Elizabeth invite the boys to join their game?
   3. Who does Melanie credit with saving the Egypt game after outsiders discover the game's existence?
   4. Why does Melanie think that Elizabeth's method is successful?

Chapter 13: "Moods and Maybes"
   1. Why does Toby's father put him on restriction?
   2. Why do Melanie's parents argue about the kids playing outside?
   3. Why is April in a bad mood?
   4. What does Caroline do to comfort April? How does it make April feel?
   5. What kind of list does Toby ask the girls to make? What does he plan to do with the list?

Chapter 14: "Hieroglyphics"
   1. What do Toby and Ken bring to Egypt?
   2. Who is Thoth?
   3. Why does Toby think they should finish the alphabet of hieroglyphics?
   4. What do the players want to purchase with the money they earn?
   5. List the players' Egyptian names and hieroglyphic symbols.
   6. Who is Petey?

Egypt Game Study Questions Page 4

Chapter 15: "The Ceremony for the Dead"
 1. What happens to Prince Pete-ho-tep?
 2. How are the high priests of Anubis chosen for the ceremony?
 3. How long does Toby think the mummification ceremony might take?
 4. Who is the chief mourner?
 5. Why do the players become less cautious?
 6. What knowledge does "one very small Egyptian" keep to himself?

Chapter 16: "The Oracle of Thoth"
 1. What do the players discuss in Egypt after school?
 2. What gets them interested in the topic of oracles?
 3. Who comes up with the idea of using Thoth as the oracle?
 4. Who asks the first question?
 5. Why does Ken think the rest of the players are crazy?

Chapter 17: "The Oracle Speaks"
 1. Who performs the ceremony of Returning to the Oracle for the Answer?
 2. What does Ken ask the oracle?
 3. Why do the Egyptians argue about the oracle's answer?

Chapter 18: "Where is Security?"
 1. What does Marshall leave in Egypt?
 2. What does April ask the oracle?
 3. How do the Egyptians react to the oracle's answer?
 4. What does Marshall ask the oracle?
 5. Who is most worried about Marshall's question to the oracle?

Chapter 19: "Confession and Confusion"
 1. Why does Toby call April at home?
 2. Why does Toby fake injury?
 3. What does Toby confess to April and Melanie?
 4. How does the oracle answer Marshall's question?
 5. Why was everyone surprised by the oracle's response to Marshall's question?

Chapter 20: "Fear Strikes"
 1. Who wants to ask the oracle another question?
 2. Why are Marshall and April alone at the Rosses' apartment?
 3. Why do Marshall and April go to Egypt alone?
 4. What happens to April after she climbs through the board in the fence?
 5. What does April wonder about Marshall's behavior as she is being attacked?
 6. Who finally calls for help?
 7. What happens to April's attacker?

Egypt Game Study Questions Page 5

Chapter 21: "The Hero"
   1. Where do Marshall and April go after leaving Egypt?
   2. Who is Inspector Grant?
   3. How does Marshall describe the man who grabs April?
   4. Who does Marshall identify as the man who called for help?
   5. What does April call Caroline for the first time?
   6. Who is the man who commits the crimes?
   7. How does Marshall's participation in the capture change his behavior?

Chapter 22: "Gains and Losses"
   1. What happens to the land of Egypt after April is attacked?
   2. What is the Professor's real name?
   3. Who begins working at the Professor's store?
   4. What objects does the Professor show to April?
   5. To whom did the items the Professor showed April once belong?
   6. How does April respond to Dorothea's letter?

Chapter 23: "Christmas Keys"
   1. Who asks to see the Egypt gang on Christmas Eve?
   2. What reason does the Professor give for wanting to meet with the group?
   3. What is the Professor's former profession?
   4. How did A-Z store get started?
   5. What information does the Professor give about the oracle?
   6. What does the Professor give to each member of the Egypt gang?
   7. What are the Professor's plans for the future?
   8. Why does April feel sad after the children receive their keys?
   9. What question does April pose to Melanie at the end of the novel?

ANSWER KEY- SHORT ANSWER STUDY GUIDE QUESTIONS - *The Egypt Game*

Chapter 1: "The Discovery of Egypt"
1. Who owns the curio store?
    The Professor owns the curio store.
2. Where is the store located?
    It is located on Orchard Avenue in a university town in California.
3. How do people in the community generally feel about the Professor?
    They fear him, though they aren't sure why.
4. Who first witnesses the Egypt Game?
    The Professor watches from inside his store.
5. What are the names of the three children the Professor watches through the window?
    The children's names are April, Melanie, and Marshall.
6. What is Marshall carrying with him?
    Marshall carries his plush octopus named Security with him.

Chapter 2: "Enter April"
1. What does April Hall sometimes call herself?
    She sometimes refers to herself as "April Dawn."
2. What is the name of the building where April comes to live?
    April moves into the Casa Rosada.
3. Who is Dorothea?
    Dorothea is April's mother.
4. Who is Caroline?
    Caroline is April's paternal grandmother.
5. What happened to April's father?
    He died in an accident before she had a chance to know him.
6. Where does Caroline work?
    Caroline works at the university library.
7. Who is April supposed to "check in" with before leaving the building?
    Caroline asks her to let the Rosses (another family in the building) know if she decides to leave the building, but she does not do so the first time she leaves.
8. What does April purchase from the drug store?
    April buys false eyelashes, in addition to a few other items.
9. Why is April impressed by the man at A-Z?
    He is able to pull off a deadpan expression during his conversation with April.
10. What does April tell the man she wants to be when she grows up?
    She explains that she would like to become an archaeologist.

Chapter 3: "Enter Melanie–and Marshall"
1. Why is Melanie hopeful as she knocks on Apartment 312?
    She believes she might make friends with the new girl who lives there.
2. What is Melanie's initial reaction when April opens the door?
    She is speechless because of April's over-the-top appearance.
3. Why doesn't April think Melanie will like her?
    Kids usually don't like April.
4. How does April first describe her mother's job to Melanie?
    April says she is a singer in the movies and travels regularly.
5. What does April learn about Mrs. Ross from her smile?
    "She wasn't going to be easy to snow."
6. What is Melanie's "favorite occupation?"
    Reading is Melanie's favorite occupation.
7. What makes April finally take off her eyelashes?
    They interfere with her ability to read; she can't see the words in the book.
8. What does Melanie keep hidden in the "dull-looking old geography book?"
    She keeps paper people that she plays with by herself.
9. How does April react to Melanie's secret hobby?
    She has a "scornful look" at first. Soon, though, she excitedly asks Melanie about each doll and joins her game.
10. What name does Melanie give to the games that the girls play?
    She calls them "imagining games."

Chapter 4: "The Egypt Girls"
1. Where do Melanie and April go almost every day in August?
    The girls go to the library every day and read about ancient Egypt.
2. How do April and Melanie earn the name "the Egypt girls?"
    They spend so much time and energy studying ancient Egypt and looking for information about ancient Egypt that they earn the name "the Egypt girls."
3. Why are April and Melanie worried about the start of school?
    April is worried that she will have a hard time fitting in at her new school; she is also worried because she has not heard from Dorothea in a month. Melanie is worried that April's Hollywood act will turn the students at Wilson off.
4. What aspect of April's appearance most concerns Melanie?
    Melanie is most worried about the impression April's false eyelashes will give to the other students.
5. What reason does April give Melanie for her feelings about Caroline?
    April believes that Caroline doesn't like Dorothea. She is also angry that Caroline seems doubtful that Dorothea will send for her to come "home" soon.
6. What do April, Marshall, and Melanie find in the deserted yard that April considers "a beautiful messenger from out of the ancient past?"
    They find an old bust of Nefertiti in the shed.

Chapter 5: "The Evil God and the Secret Spy"
1. Who does Melanie suggest might be watching them through the window?
    She thinks the Professor may be watching since the yard is officially his property. The girls are relieved to discover the window is covered with a thick curtain and a thick layer of dirt.
2. Who do the girls appoint pharaoh?
    Marshall is named the pharaoh, who will inherit the throne of Egypt.
3. What do they name the pharaoh?
    They call him Marshamosis, which they deem a more appropriate title for a pharaoh of ancient Egypt.
4. Why does Marshall agree to play the game?
    He agrees to play after Melanie and April explain that the pharaoh was king over all of Egypt–and gave orders that everyone had to follow.
5. Who is Set?
    Set is the god of evil and black magic.
6. Where do the girls get the rules for the Egypt game?
    They make them up as they play–(extemporaneous and impromptu).
7. What happens–unbeknownst to the girls–after they throw the boxes over the fence?
    The curtain on the inside of the dirty window is pushed aside to clear the view for someone inside the store.

Chapter 6: "Eyelashes and Ceremony"
1. Why is April having trouble concentrating the day before school is to begin?
    She is thinking about the first day of school and remembering that Dorothea promised to bring her home soon.
2. Why is Melanie having trouble concentrating?
    She is worried about pulling off her plan to take April's eyelashes.
3. What does Melanie take from April's room? How?
    She manages to take the eyelashes by swiping her hand quickly over them. The adhesive holds them fast to her hands.
4. How do the sixth graders at Wilson respond to April?
    After a few weeks, though they remain a little standoffish, they become proud of her uniqueness.
5. What nickname do Toby and Ken give to April? Why is it important?
    They start calling her February, which shows she has been accepted by the Wilson students as one of their own.
6. What do Isis and Nefertiti represent?
    They stand for love, beauty, and perfection.
7. How are the rituals of the Egypt game recorded?
    First the players write them down on notebook paper. Soon, though, they choose onionskin paper rolled on pieces of an old fishing pole in imitation of ancient papyrus scrolls.

8. What is the Crocodile Stone? What do the girls do with it?
    The Crocodile Stone is a rock Melanie mysteriously finds on the sidewalk. It is shaped much like a crocodile, so they place it on the altar of Set and attribute Set's power to it.
9. Why does Mr. Ross believe that Marshall depends on Security?
    He claims that being a baby offended Marshall's dignity.

Chapter 7: "Neferbeth"
1. Who moves into Casa Rosada in September? How old is she?
    Elizabeth Chung moves into the building with her two sisters and her widowed mother. Elizabeth is nine years old.
2. What subjects is Mr. Ross preparing to teach?
    He is studying to teach college literature and poetry.
3. Who does Elizabeth look like to April and Melanie?
    She reminds them of Nefertiti.
4. Why do April and Melanie ask Elizabeth to join the Egypt game?
    Once they realize how much she resembles Nefertiti, they cannot help but include her in their game.

Chapter 8: "Prisoners of Fear"
1. How does Elizabeth respond to the Egypt Game?
    She loves everything about it and constantly compliments April and Melanie on their ideas.
2. What name do Melanie and April give to Elizabeth in the game?
    They call her Neferbeth.
3. What puts a temporary stop to the Egypt game?
    A little girl in the neighborhood is killed. She is the second child in a year to be murdered, and the murderer is suspected to live in the neighborhood. Everyone is petrified since no arrests have been made, so they will not allow the children to play in the neighborhood unsupervised.
4. Who does the community begin to believe is guilty?
    They begin to suspect the Professor, though they have no evidence.
5. Who organizes the efforts to invite the Professor to leave?
    Mr. Schmitt, the owner of Schmitt's Variety Store, encourages others in the community to write letters and sign petitions asking the Professor to leave.
6. How do the players continue the Egypt game when they are confined to the Casa Rosada?
    They gather supplies from around the apartment complex to create costumes for themselves.
7. How do accusations against the Professor affect his business?
    People from the community no longer visit his store at all.
8. What weighs on April's mind when she doesn't have the Egypt Game to occupy her time?
    The absence of her mother's letters and Dorothea's avoidance of April's many questions concerning her eventual return to Hollywood.

9. What changes do the players notice in Egypt when they stop by briefly?
    The Crocodile Stone has shifted position a little, and the flowers seem to stay fresh, though the Egypt gang has not been by to replace them.

Chapter 9: "Summoned by the Mighty Ones"
1. Under what circumstances are the kids in the neighborhood allowed to trick-or-treat?
    They are chaperoned by some of the fathers.
2. What is April's plan for revisiting Egypt?
    She thinks they should separate from the large trick-or-treating group when the chaperones are not looking.
3. What costumes do April, Elizabeth, Melanie, and Marshall wear for Halloween?
    They wear the Egyptian costumes they created while they were not allowed to play alone in Egypt.
4. What token does April claim Set and Isis have sent to the players as a summons?
    They send a shiny bird feather.
5. What are the players watching for as they trick-or-treat?
    They watch for a secret omen that will cue them to return to Egypt.

Chapter 10: "The Return to Egypt"
1. Why does Marshall ask to hold a sign as he is standing with the other trick-or-treaters?
    Marshall confuses the trick-or-treaters with a gathering of university demonstrators that he has observed in the past.
2. Who do the girls run into while trick-or-treating?
    They see Toby Alvillar and Ken Kamata, the two boys in April's and Melanie's class who gave April her nickname.
3. Describe Toby's and Ken's costumes.
    Toby is "The New American," an idea that his artist father developed and created with many product boxes tied to Toby. Ken is wearing a store-bought monster costume, complete with rubber mask, hands, and feet.
4. What does the Egypt gang claim as the secret omen?
    The gang sees a shooting star, which April confirms as the "secret omen."

Chapter 11: "Egypt Invaded"
1. What does April declare the Crocodile God demands for sacrifice?
    He demands Security.
2. What does Marshall mumble under his breath after April tells him not to yell?
    He claims that "somebody already heard us."
3. What do the players decide to use for sacrifice?
    Each of them chooses a hair or piece of fingernail to sacrifice.
4. What happens at the end of the Ceremony of Sacrifice?
    An intruder lands in Egypt as the players conclude their ceremony.

Chapter 12: "Elizabethan Diplomacy"
1. Who enters Egypt uninvited?
    Ken and Toby jump over the fence without invitation.
2. Why does Elizabeth invite the boys to join their game?
    She hopes it will keep them from telling an adult about their secret Egypt.
3. Who does Melanie credit with saving the Egypt game after outsiders discover the game's existence?
    Melanie attributes the save to Elizabeth's diplomacy.
4. Why does Melanie think that Elizabeth's method was successful?
    Elizabeth's diplomacy appeals to the boys' better natures. Mrs. Ross has explained to Melanie that non-violent demonstrations operate according to the same principle in order to effect change.

Chapter 13: "Moods and Maybes"
1. Why does Toby's father put him on restriction?
    Toby's costume, which his father spent a great deal of time and energy making, is destroyed on Halloween.
2. Why do Melanie's parents argue about the kids playing outside?
    Mr. Ross believes they shouldn't keep them inside indefinitely, while Mrs. Ross disagrees out of concern for their safety (the murderer is still at large and unidentified). Finally, they reach a compromise: Melanie and Marshall can play outside as long as someone plays with them.
3. Why is April in a bad mood?
    A letter from Dorothea announces Dorothea's marriage to Nick. Dorothea also tells her she will be sending all of April's belongings to Caroline's instead of bringing April home to live with them.
4. What does Caroline do to comfort April? How does it make April feel?
    She offers a squeeze on the shoulder, a kiss on the top of the head, and then leaves April alone. April feels a little better afterward.
5. What kind of list does Toby ask the girls to make? What does he plan to do with the list?
    Toby wants a list of the best books about Egypt because he is planning to go to the library to research Egypt later that evening.

Chapter 14: "Hieroglyphics"
1. What do Toby and Ken bring to Egypt?
    The pair brings items for evil Set's altar, including a shrunken head and a large stuffed owl.
2. Who is Thoth?
    Because Toby brings an owl that has been stuffed, it reminds someone in the group of the "bird-headed god of wisdom and writing" named Thoth. Consequently, they give the owl the name of Thoth.
3. Why does Toby think they should finish the alphabet of hieroglyphics?
    The finished alphabet would offer the players a way to communicate about Egypt while at school and in the community without giving away their secret Egypt.

4. What do the players want to purchase with the money they earn?
   They want to better imitate the magical art form of ancient hieroglyphics, and they feel that colored pens will improve their authenticity.
5. List the players' Egyptian names and hieroglyphic symbols.
   (See novel for symbols)
   Toby- RAMOSE   April- BASTET
   Ken- HOREMHEB   Elizabeth- NEFERTITI (NEFERBETH)
   Melanie- AIDA   Marshall- MARSHAMOSIS
6. Who is Petey?
   Petey is Elizabeth's pet parakeet that dies.

Chapter 15: "The Ceremony for the Dead"
1. What happens to Prince Pete-ho-tep?
   He is killed by a cat.
2. How are the high priests of Anubis chosen for the ceremony?
   Elizabeth, as owner of the parakeet, places a pebble in her hand for random selection. Since Toby and Ken correctly choose the hand with the pebble, they are made the high priests.
3. How long does Toby think the mummification ceremony might take?
   He claims it could last five or six days.
4. Who is the chief mourner?
   Elizabeth is chief mourner since the parakeet was her pet.
5. Why do the players become less cautious?
   They feel much more at home in Egypt, so as they become increasingly excited about their activities, they start talking in normal tones, forgetting the measures they should be taking to remain quiet and protect Egypt's secrecy.
6. What knowledge does "one very small Egyptian" keep to himself?
   He knows that the Land of Egypt is being watched.

Chapter 16: "The Oracle of Thoth"
1. What do the players discuss in Egypt after school?
   They talk about the "What and How of the Egyptian oracle."
2. What gets them interested in the topic of oracles?
   Their interest is piqued by a discussion about oracles in Mrs. Granger's sixth grade class.
3. Who comes up with the idea of using Thoth as the oracle?
   Toby proposes using Thoth, the Egyptian God of Wisdom, for authenticity.
4. Who asks the first question to the oracle?
   Ken draws the first straw and poses the first question to the oracle.
5. Why does Ken think the rest of the Egypt players are crazy?
   He is shocked that they might believe their questions actually will be answered by some mysterious oracle.

Chapter 17: "The Oracle Speaks"
1. Who performs the ceremony of Returning to the Oracle for the Answer?
    Bastet/April performs the ceremony.
2. What does Ken ask the oracle?
    He wants to know: "Will I be a big league star someday?"
3. Why do the Egyptians argue about the oracle's answer?
    They all believe that one of them has answered Ken's question, but they cannot determine whom, which frustrates them because they all pledged not to tamper with the process.

Chapter 18: "Where is Security?"
1. What does Marshall leave in Egypt?
    He leaves Security.
2. What does April ask the oracle?
    She asks: "When will I go home again?"
3. How do the Egyptians react to the oracle's answer?
    They do not believe that one of the kids could have written the answer, and they are not sure what to make of it.
4. What does Marshall ask the oracle?
    He asks: "Where is Security?"
5. Who is most worried about Marshall's question?
    Toby is more concerned about Marshall and his question than anyone else.

Chapter 19: "Confession and Confusion"
1. Why does Toby call April at home?
    He hopes to set up a meeting at school the next day because he is struggling with his conscience.
2. Why does Toby fake injury?
    He wants to break away from the guys playing basketball at recess in order to sneak in a conversation with April and Melanie.
3. What does Toby confess to April and Melanie?
    He admits that he has been acting as the oracle, but he doesn't know what to do about Marshall.
4. How does the oracle answer Marshall's question?
    The paper reads, "Look under the throne of Set."
5. Why is everyone surprised by the oracle's response to Marshall's question?
    They are surprised because Toby admitted that he did not know where Security is, yet Security is found under the throne of Set, just as the oracle indicates.

Chapter 20: "Fear Strikes"
1. Who wants to ask the oracle another question?
    April wants someone to ask another question.
2. Why are Marshall and April alone at the Rosses' apartment?
    April is staying with Marshall while Melanie and her parents attend a concert.

3. Why do Marshall and April go to Egypt alone?
   April wants to retrieve her math book, which she has left there accidentally, in order to complete her homework.
4. What happens to April after she climbs through the board in the fence?
   Someone grabs her when she isn't paying attention.
5. What does April wonder about Marshall's behavior as she is being attacked?
   She wonders why he isn't calling for help.
6. Who finally calls for help?
   A strange voice (which they later realize is the Professor's voice) calls for help.
7. What happens to April's attacker?
   He runs away when he hears someone call for help.

Chapter 21:"The Hero"
1. Where do Marshall and April go after leaving Egypt?
   They are taken to the police station.
2. Who is Inspector Grant?
   He is the policeman who asks the most questions about April's attack.
3. How does Marshall describe the man who grabs April?
   Marshall states that he is a "big man,"–"old"–with "orange hair and spotted skin."
4. Who does Marshall identify as the man who called for help?
   He tells police that the Professor called for help and saved April.
5. What does April call Caroline for the first time?
   She calls her "Grandma" and asks to go home–to Caroline's apartment.
6. Who is the man who commits the crimes?
   He is Mr. Schmitt's relative who sometimes works in his variety store.
7. How does Marshall's participation in the capture of the attacker change his behavior?
   He no longer takes Security with him everywhere he goes.

Chapter 22: "Gains and Losses"
1. What happens to the land of Egypt after April is attacked?
   It is boarded up.
2. What is the Professor's real name?
   The Professor's real name is Dr. Huddleston.
3. Who begins working at the Professor's store?
   Elizabeth's mother, Mrs. Chung, takes a job at the store following April's attack.
4. What objects does the Professor show to April?
   He reveals a small head of alabaster and a flat piece of marble facing from the wall of a tomb, which is marked with hieroglyphics.
5. To whom did the items the Professor showed April once belong?
   Dr. Huddleston tells April they once belonged to his deceased wife, Anne.
6. How does April respond to Dorothea's letter?
   She declines the invitation to visit Dorothea at Christmas, explaining, "Grandma and I have our plans all made for Christmas Eve."

Chapter 23: "Christmas Keys"
1. Who asks to see the Egypt gang on Christmas Eve?
    The Professor wants to meet with the players.
2. What reason does the Professor give for wanting to meet with the group?
    He has come to tell them a story.
3. What is the Professor's former profession?
    He was a Professor of anthropology at the university.
4. How did A-Z store get started?
    Anne, the Professor's deceased wife, had the idea to start it in order to sell some of the handmade crafts from the native peoples with whom she worked and studied.
5. What information does the Professor give about the oracle?
    The professor answered the question Marshall posed to the oracle because he wanted Marshall to be able to find his beloved Security.
6. What does the Professor give to each member of the Egypt gang?
    He hands them each a key to the padlock that has been put in place to protect Egypt.
7. What are the Professor's plans for the future?
    He will begin importing, traveling, and selling goods again.
8. Why does April feel sad after the children receive their keys?
    She fears they will return to Egypt with high expectations, but will end up being disappointed and ruin the "remembering."
9. What question does April pose to Melanie at the end of the novel?
    "Melanie, what do you know about Gypsies?"

STUDY GUIDE/QUIZ QUESTIONS - *The Egypt Game*
Multiple Choice Format

Chapter 1: "The Discovery of Egypt"

1. Who owns the curio store?
    A. the state of California
    B. the Professor
    C. Nefertiti
    D. the university
2. Where is the store located?
    A. on Orchard Avenue in California
    B. at a booth of the state fair
    C. at the University of California
    D. New York City
3. How do people in the community generally feel about the Professor?
    A. They love and respect him.
    B. They take advantage of him.
    C. They fear him.
    D. They believe he is dishonest.
4. Who first witnesses the Egypt Game?
    A. a five-year-old little girl
    B. the Professor
    C. Nefertiti's son
    D. Melanie's grandmother
5. What are the names of the three children the Professor watches through the window?
    A. Melanie, April, and Marshall
    B. Melanie, Peter, and Ken
    C. Peter, Ken, and Marshall
    D. Marshall, Dorothea, and April
6. What does Marshall carry with him?
    A. a flashlight
    B. his lunch
    C. a blanket
    D. a stuffed octopus

Egypt Game Multiple Choice Questions Page 2

Chapter 2: "Enter April"
1. What does April Hall sometimes call herself?
    A. Queen April
    B. Super Sleuth
    C. Nefertiti
    D. April Dawn
2. What is the name of the building where April comes to live?
    A. the Hilton
    B. California Detention Center
    C. Casa Rosada
    D. The Curio Store
3. Who is Dorothea?
    A. April's mother
    B. April's grandmother
    C. April's cat
    D. April's aunt
4. Who is Caroline?
    A. April's best friend
    B. April's grandmother
    C. April's cat
    D. April's mother
5. What happened to April's father?
    A. He was arrested.
    B. He got lost on the interstate.
    C. He broke his thumb.
    D. He died in an accident before April knew him.
6. Where does Caroline work?
    A. at the curio store
    B. at the grocery store
    C. at the University library
    D. at the drug store
7. Who is April supposed to "check in" with before leaving the building?
    A. the Rosses
    B. the front desk receptionist
    C. a police officer
    D. Caroline
8. What does April purchase from the drugstore?
    A. a heating pad
    B. lipstick
    C. false eyelashes
    D. a magazine

Egypt Game Multiple Choice Questions Page 3

9. Why is April impressed by the man at A-Z?
    A. He has a deadpan expression.
    B. He has so many beautiful things.
    C. He knows her name.
    D. He is a famous movie star.
10. What does April tell the man she wants to be when she grows up?
    A. an actress
    B. Miss America
    C. a doctor
    D. an archaeologist

Egypt Game Multiple Choice Questions Page 4

Chapter 3: "Enter Melanie–and Marshall"
1. Why is Melanie hopeful as she knocks on Apartment 312?
    A. She might meet a new friend.
    B. She expects a surprise party.
    C. She thinks Dorothea will be there.
    D. She is lost and hopes to get directions back to her house.
2. What is Melanie's initial reaction when April opens the door?
    A. She is frightened and starts to tremble.
    B. She laughs at the scene before her.
    C. She is speechless.
    D. She becomes angry.
3. Why doesn't April think Melanie will like her?
    A. Kids usually don't like April.
    B. They have always fought with one another.
    C. They are rivals on opposite soccer teams.
    D. They have nothing in common.
4. How does April first describe her mother's job to Melanie?
    A. She explains that she works overtime at their hometown mill.
    B. She is a struggling artist hoping to make it big.
    C. She is a singer in the movies and travels regularly.
    D. She is unemployed.
5. What does April learn about Mrs. Ross from her smile?
    A. She has no teeth.
    B. She is a fun person, quick to laugh.
    C. She isn't easy to fool.
    D. She is a pleasant conversationalist.
6. What is Melanie's "favorite occupation?"
    A. singing
    B. archaeology
    C. playing the piano
    D. reading
7. What makes April finally take off her eyelashes?
    A. Her teacher doesn't allow her to wear them.
    B. They make reading difficult.
    C. She loses one of them.
    D. She decides to wear sunglasses instead.
8. What does Melanie keep hidden in the "dull-looking old geography book?"
    A. old letters
    B. a diary
    C. stickers
    D. paper people

Egypt Game Multiple Choice Questions Page 5

9. How does April react to Melanie's secret hobby?
   A. She storms out of the room.
   B. She admires it.
   C. She joins in the activity with Melanie.
   D. She begins to laugh.
10. What name does Melanie give to the games that the girls play?
    A. impromptu
    B. imagining games
    C. artistic license
    D. Egyptian antics

Egypt Game Multiple Choice Questions Page 6

Chapter 4: "The Egypt Girls"
1. Where do Melanie and April go almost everyday in August?
    A. movie theater
    B. library
    C. skating rink
    D. into the curio shop
2. How do April and Melanie earn the name "the Egypt girls?"
    A. They win a costume contest.
    B. That is the name of their band.
    C. They are both from Egypt.
    D. They spend so much time and energy studying ancient Egypt.
3. Why are April and Melanie worried about the start of school?
    A. They have the most feared teacher in the school.
    B. They are afraid April won't fit in at Wilson.
    C. They will not see each other for three months.
    D. They will have to attend separate schools.
4. What aspect of April's appearance most concerns Melanie?
    A. April's funky outfits
    B. April's purple boots
    C. April's false eyelashes
    D. April's upswept hair
5. What reason does April give Melanie for her feelings about Caroline?
    A. She appreciates the fact that Caroline allows her to stay with her.
    B. She had never met Caroline before coming to the Casa Rosada.
    C. Caroline is a mean and stingy woman.
    D. Caroline does not like Dorothea and doesn't believe Dorothea will send for her.
6. What found item does April consider "a beautiful messenger from out of the ancient past?"
    A. an old bust of Nefertiti
    B. a statue of Napolean
    C. a sculpture of a pigeon
    D. an old leather travel journal

Egypt Game Multiple Choice Questions Page 7

Chapter 5: "The Evil God and the Secret Spy"
1. Who does Melanie suggest might be watching them through the window?
	A. Caroline
	B. Marshall
	C. the Professor
	D. her parents
2. Who do the girls appoint as pharaoh?
	A. Marshall
	B. Nefertiti
	C. the Professor
	D. King Tut
3. What name do they give the pharaoh?
	A. Thoth
	B. the Sphinx
	C. Marsha
	D. Marshamosis
4. Why does Marshall agree to play the game?
	A. He discovers that the pharaoh was king over all of Egypt.
	B. The girls promise him a candy bar.
	C. He is bored.
	D. He wants to prove to the girls that he isn't too little to play.
5. Who is Set?
	A. the god of wisdom and intellect
	B. the god of beauty and love
	C. the god of humor and laughter
	D. the god of evil and black magic
6. Where do the girls get the rules for the Egypt game?
	A. The girls found them on a scroll hidden in the bust of Nefertiti.
	B. They invent them as they play.
	C. They got a book of rules from the library.
	D. Mr. Ross outlines the rules.
7. What happens–unbeknownst to the girls–after they throw the boxes over the fence?
	A. Someone runs away with the boxes.
	B. Someone moves aside the curtain and looks out the window.
	C. Marshall runs away.
	D. Caroline comes looking for them.

Egypt Game Multiple Choice Questions Page 8

Chapter 6: "Eyelashes and Ceremony"
1. Why is April having trouble concentrating the day before school is to begin?
    A. She has the flu.
    B. She is getting ready to move to another state.
    C. She is remembering that Dorothea promised to bring her home soon.
    D. She is too excited about making new friends.
2. Why is Melanie having trouble concentrating the day before school begins?
    A. She is worried about pulling off her plan to take April's eyelashes.
    B. She is worried about cheerleading try-outs.
    C. She is afraid of her new teacher.
    D. She isn't having trouble concentrating.
3. What does Melanie take from April's room?
    A. hairbrush
    B. eyelashes
    C. a letter
    D. April's diary
4. How do the sixth graders at Wilson respond to April?
    A. They ridicule and mock her.
    B. They love her immediately.
    C. They remain a little standoffish but become proud of her uniqueness.
    D. They don't notice her.
5. What nickname do Toby and Ken give to April?
    A. February
    B. spider eyes
    C. Nefertiti
    D. Prima Donna
6. What do Isis and Nefertiti represent?
    A. faith and hope
    B. wisdom and intellect
    C. love, beauty, and perfection
    D. strength and devotion
7. How are the rituals of the Egypt game recorded?
    A. with a tape recorder
    B. on onionskin paper rolled on pieces of an old fishing pole
    C. in April's diary
    D. nowhere
8. What is the Crocodile Stone?
    A. a rock Melanie finds and places on the altar of Set
    B. an artifact from the A-Z shop
    C. Caroline's favorite piece of jewelry
    D. Marshall's favorite movie

Egypt Game Multiple Choice Questions Page 9

9. Why does Marshall's dad say Marshall needs Security?
    A. because he gets cold
    B. because he's lonely
    C. because being a baby offends Marshall's dignity
    D. because it is the only toy Marshall owns

Egypt Game Multiple Choice Questions Page 10

Chapter 7: "Neferbeth"
1. Who moves into Casa Rosada in September?
	A. the Chung family (including nine-year old Elizabeth)
	B. the Martin family (including ten-year old Sam)
	C. Dorothea
	D. Thoth
2. What subjects is Mr. Ross preparing to teach?
	A. college math and science
	B. college literature and poetry
	C. kindergarten and preschool
	D. drivers' education and social studies
3. Who does Elizabeth look like to April and Melanie?
	A. Miss America
	B. Nefertiti
	C. another friend from the Casa Rosada
	D. April's mother
4. Why do April and Melanie ask Elizabeth to join the Egypt game?
	A. They have to have one more player in order to play properly.
	B. They have to take care of her in the afternoons.
	C. She looks so much like Nefertiti that they cannot help but include her in their game.
	D. Elizabeth threatens to tattle on them if they don't.

Egypt Game Multiple Choice Questions Page 11

Chapter 8: "Prisoners of Fear"

1. How does Elizabeth respond to the Egypt Game?
    A. It frightens her.
    B. She loves it.
    C. She is bored by it.
    D. She quits after one day.
2. What name do Melanie and April give to Elizabeth in the game?
    A. Baby Beth
    B. Neferbeth
    C. Cleopatra
    D. Isis
3. What puts a temporary stop to the Egypt game?
    A. April gets the flu.
    B. The Rosses go on vacation.
    C. There is a snow storm.
    D. A child is murdered in the neighborhood.
4. Who does the community begin to believe is guilty?
    A. Mr. Ross
    B. the Professor
    C. the Mayor
    D. the janitor at the Casa Rosada
5. Who organizes the efforts to invite the Professor to leave the community?
    A. Mr. Schmitt
    B. Caroline
    C. Dorothea
    D. The Rosses
6. How do the players continue the Egypt game when they are confined to the Casa Rosada?
    A. They don't.
    B. They use the basement.
    C. They gather supplies from around the apartment complex to create costumes.
    D. They watch movies about Egypt.
7. How do accusations against the Professor affect his business?
    A. It helps by bringing in customers.
    B. People from the community no longer visit his store at all.
    C. It doesn't affect his business.
    D. He loses his shop altogether.
8. What weighs on April's mind when she doesn't have the Egypt Game to occupy her time?
    A. fear the murderer might strike again
    B. the absence of her mother's letters
    C. a fight with Melanie
    D. the way the kids at her school treat her

Egypt Game Multiple Choice Questions Page 12

9. What changes do the players notice in Egypt when they stop by briefly?
   A. There are no changes.
   B. Everything has been cleared away.
   C. The Crocodile Stone has shifted a little and the flowers remain fresh.
   D. A stage has been built in the yard.

Egypt Game Multiple Choice Questions Page 13

Chapter 9: "Summoned by the Mighty Ones"
1. Under what circumstances are the kids in the neighborhood allowed to trick-or-treat?
    A. They are chaperoned by some of the fathers.
    B. They may only trick-or-treat inside the apartment complex.
    C. The murderer has been arrested.
    D. The kids are accompanied by a policeman.
2. What is April's plan for revisiting Egypt?
    A. The Egyptians should separate from the large trick-or-treating group.
    B. She decides to tell Caroline and the Rosses about Egypt.
    C. The Egyptians should sneak out of their homes after everyone is asleep.
    D. The Egyptians should go to Egypt during school hours.
3. What costumes do April, Elizabeth, Melanie, and Marshall wear for Halloween?
    A. characters from *The Wizard of Oz*
    B. Egyptian costumes they created
    C. costumes the Professor gave them from his shop
    D. costumes Mrs. Ross and Caroline made for them
4. What token does April claim Set and Isis have sent to the players as a summons?
    A. a shiny quarter
    B. a shiny silver earring
    C. a shiny bird feather
    D. a shiny gold coin
5. What are the players watching for as they trick-or-treat?
    A. someone dressed as Frankenstein
    B. a funny jack-o-lantern
    C. a secret omen that will cue them to return to Egypt
    D. Marshall's Security

Egypt Game Multiple Choice Questions Page 14

Chapter 10: "The Return to Egypt"
1. Why does Marshall ask for a sign as they are standing with the other trick-or-treaters?
    A. No one knows what his costume is, so he wants to wear a sign.
    B. He confuses the trick-or-treaters with a gathering of university demonstrators.
    C. He is looking for the beginning of the line, marked with a "start" sign.
    D. He is asking for the secret omen to appear.
2. Who do the girls run into while trick-or-treating?
    A. the Professor
    B. Dorothea
    C. Toby Alvillar and Ken Kamata
    D. Caroline
3. What are Toby and Ken dressed as?
    A. knights of King Arthur's court
    B. peanut butter and jelly
    C. Charlie Brown and Snoopy
    D. "The New American" and a monster
4. What does the Egypt gang claim as the secret omen?
    A. a funny jack-o-lantern
    B. a shooting star
    C. a bag full of Tootsie Rolls
    D. a full moon

Egypt Game Multiple Choice Questions Page 15

Chapter 11: "Egypt Invaded"
1. What does April declare the Crocodile God demands for sacrifice?
    A. a Snickers bar
    B. a turkey sandwich
    C. Security
    D. April's false eyelashes
2. What does Marshall mumble under his breath after April tells him not to yell?
    A. "I wasn't yelling."
    B. "You're not my boss."
    C. "Somebody already heard us."
    D. "Well, you were yelling, too."
3. What do the players decide to use for sacrifice?
    A. their trick-or-treat loot
    B. hair or a piece of fingernail
    C. a half-rotten pumpkin
    D. a piece of jewelry
4. What happens at the end of the ceremony of sacrifice?
    A. It begins to rain.
    B. The statue of Set falls over.
    C. April stubs her toe.
    D. An intruder lands in Egypt.

Egypt Game Multiple Choice Questions Page 16

Chapter 12: "Elizabethan Diplomacy"
1. Who enters Egypt uninvited?
	A. Ken and Toby
	B. a stray cat
	C. Elizabeth's two sisters
	D. Melanie's parents
2. Why does Elizabeth invite the boys to join their game?
	A. She has to, to keep them from telling an adult about Egypt.
	B. They have been wanting some more male actors.
	C. She has a crush on Toby.
	D. She asks the boys to join before she even thinks about it.
3. Who does Melanie credit with saving the Egypt game after outsiders discover the game's existence?
	A. the Professor
	B. Set
	C. Elizabeth
	D. Marshall
4. Why does Melanie think that Elizabeth's method was successful?
	A. because the boys really wanted to be friends
	B. because it appealed to the boys' better natures
	C. because the boys had nothing else to do after school
	D. because she blackmailed the boys with a secret

Egypt Game Multiple Choice Questions Page 17

Chapter 13: "Moods and Maybes"
1. Why does Toby's father put him on restriction?
	A. for sneaking out of the house
	B. for stealing candy from the drug store
	C. for destroying his Halloween costume
	D. for failing math
2. Why do Melanie's parents argue about the kids playing outside?
	A. Mr. Ross wants them to go to the playground, and Mrs. Ross votes for soccer.
	B. Mr. Ross wants them to play while Mrs. Ross wants them to finish their homework.
	C. Mr. Ross wants them to play outside, but Mrs. Ross is concerned for their safety.
	D. Mr. Ross thinks they should go outside, but Mrs. Ross wants them to clean their rooms.
3. Why is April in a bad mood?
	A. A letter from Dorothea depresses her.
	B. She has the flu.
	C. She loses her favorite book.
	D. She loses a spelling bee.
4. What does Caroline do to comfort April?
	A. She makes some soup.
	B. She takes April to the movies.
	C. She offers April a squeeze on the shoulder and a kiss on the head.
	D. She tells her a story about her own childhood experiences.
5. What kind of list does Toby ask the girls to make?
	A. a list of all the kids in the class with their phone numbers
	B. a list of the best books about Egypt
	C. a list of pizza places in the neighborhood
	D. a list of the funniest movies they have ever seen

Egypt Game Multiple Choice Questions Page 18

Chapter 14: "Hieroglyphics"
1. What do Toby and Ken bring to Egypt?
    A. items for evil Set's altar, including a shrunken head and a large stuffed owl
    B. their sleeping bags
    C. potato chips and sodas
    D. two of their best friends
2. Who is Thoth?
    A. Ken's grandfather
    B. the bird-headed god of wisdom and writing
    C. the local comedian
    D. Melanie's father
3. Why does Toby think they should finish the alphabet of hieroglyphics?
    A. so they can make t-shirts with it
    B. so they can make copies for their class at school
    C. as extra-credit for social studies
    D. so they can use it as a secret code outside of Egypt
4. What do the players want to purchase with the money they earn?
    A. a new book about Egypt
    B. colored pens
    C. an umbrella
    D. a telephone
5. Who is Petey?
    A. Toby's twin brother
    B. Melanie's cat
    C. Elizabeth's pet parakeet that dies
    D. the Professor

Egypt Game Multiple Choice Questions Page 19

Chapter 15: "The Ceremony for the Dead"
1. What happens to Prince Pete-ho-tep?
    A. He is killed by a cat.
    B. He becomes pharaoh.
    C. He disappears without explanation
    D. He drowns
2. How are the high priests of Anubis chosen for the ceremony?
    A. Elizabeth quizzed all candidates about ancient Egypt. The two with the most correct answers were appointed high priests.
    B. Elizabeth put a pebble in her hand and let them choose. Those who guessed correctly were appointed high priests.
    C. The oldest members were given the honor of being the high priests.
    D. They held an arm-wrestling tournament, and the winners were appointed high priests.
3. How long does Toby think the mummification ceremony might take?
    A. three hours
    B. three weeks
    C. five or six days
    D. ten minutes
4. Who is the chief mourner?
    A. Petey
    B. Elizabeth
    C. April
    D. Melanie
5. Why do the players become less cautious?
    A. They don't care if people learn about their Egypt.
    B. They feel more at home in Egypt, so they forget to be cautious.
    C. The murderer is arrested.
    D. Fewer people are around in November.
6. What knowledge does "one very small Egyptian" hold that he chooses not to share with the others?
    A. He knows that the Land of Egypt is being watched.
    B. He knows the answer to the Riddle of the Sphynx.
    C. He knows who killed Cock Robin.
    D. He learns that the chicken came before the egg.

Egypt Game Multiple Choice Questions Page 20

Chapter 16: "The Oracle of Thoth"
1. What do the players discuss in Egypt after school?
    A. how to exclude Marshall from the game
    B. plans for erecting a pyramid
    C. The Marriage Ceremony
    D. the What and How of the Egyptian oracle
2. What gets the gang interested in the topic of the oracle?
    A. a discussion about oracles in Mrs. Granger's sixth grade class
    B. a comment made by Mr. Ross
    C. an article in the newspaper
    D. a scene from a movie
3. Who comes up with the idea of using Thoth as the oracle?
    A. Toby
    B. April
    C. Melanie
    D. Elizabeth
4. Who asks the first question to the oracle?
    A. Melanie
    B. April
    C. Ken
    D. Marshall
5. Why does Ken think the rest of the Egypt players are crazy?
    A. They want to stay in Egypt overnight.
    B. They believe their questions actually will be answered by some mysterious oracle.
    C. They want to wear their Egypt costumes to school.
    D. They want to skip school to play the Egypt game.

Egypt Game Multiple Choice Questions Page 21

Chapter 17: "The Oracle Speaks"
1. Who performs the ceremony of Returning to the Oracle for the Answer?
    A. April
    B. Marshall
    C. Melanie
    D. Toby
2. What does Ken ask the oracle?
    A. "Where did I leave my wallet?"
    B. "Will I be a big league star someday?"
    C. "Will I pass my math test tomorrow?"
    D. "What will I get for my birthday?"
3. Why do the Egyptians argue about the oracle's answer?
    A. They believe that one of them has answered Ken's question.
    B. They can't read the oracle's response.
    C. They argue over how the question was asked to the oracle.
    D. They argue over whether the oracle's response can be trusted.

Egypt Game Multiple Choice Questions Page 22

Chapter 18: "Where is Security?"
1. What does Marshall leave in Egypt?
	A. his lunch
	B. Security
	C. his crayons
	D. his watch
2. What does April ask the oracle?
	A. "Where is my mother?"
	B. "Will I pass math?"
	C. "When will I go home again?"
	D. "Who will win the World Series?"
3. How do the Egyptians react to the oracle's answer?
	A. They believe one of the kids wrote the answer.
	B. They know one of the parents wrote the answer.
	C. April knows Dorothea wrote the answer.
	D. They are not sure what to make of it.
4. What does Marshall ask the oracle?
	A. "Where is Security?"
	B. "Where are my tennis shoes?"
	C. "What will I get for Christmas?"
	D. "Where will I go to elementary school?"
5. Who is most worried about Marshall's question?
	A. Melanie
	B. Ken
	C. Toby
	D. April

Egypt Game Multiple Choice Questions Page 23

Chapter 19: "Confession and Confusion"
1. Why does Toby call April at home?
   A. He wants to ask her to the movies.
   B. He has a question about his math homework.
   C. He wants to set up a meeting at school the next day.
   D. He does it as a practical joke.
2. Why does Toby fake injury?
   A. as an excuse to separate from his friends in order to talk to April and Melanie
   B. so that the coach won't make him run laps
   C. so that his teacher will feel sorry for him
   D. to make everyone laugh
3. What does Toby confess to April and Melanie?
   A. that he told his friends about Egypt
   B. that he has never liked basketball
   C. that he has been acting as the oracle, but doesn't know how to help Marshall
   D. that he lost the books about Egypt that they lent to him
4. How does the oracle answer Marshall's question?
   A. "You must look for security within yourself."
   B. "Look under the throne of Set."
   C. "Security must find his own way home."
   D. The oracle does not respond at all.
5. Why are the players surprised by the oracle's response to Marshall's question?
   A. because the oracle turns out to be right, though Toby is not responsible
   B. because they thought the oracle would be able to help Marshall
   C. because they did not believe that the oracle would ignore Marshall's question
   D. because the oracle's response is written in hieroglyphics

Egypt Game Multiple Choice Questions Page 24

Chapter 20: "Fear Strikes"

1. Who wants to ask the oracle another question?
    A. Caroline wants to ask a question.
    B. The Professor wants to ask a question.
    C. April wants someone to ask another question.
    D. Mrs. Chung wants to ask a question.
2. Why are Marshall and April alone at the Rosses' apartment?
    A. They want to work on new Egypt costumes in secret.
    B. April is staying with Marshall while Melanie and Melanie's parents attend a concert
    C. Someone is painting April's and Caroline's apartment.
    D. They are decorating for Melanie's birthday party.
3. Why do Marshall and April go to Egypt alone?
    A. April wants to retrieve her math book.
    B. They want to try a new ceremony.
    C. They want to retrieve Security.
    D. They think they are meeting the rest of the group there.
4. What happens to April after she climbs through the board in the fence?
    A. She cuts her leg on the fence.
    B. She falls into a rain puddle.
    C. Someone grabs her when she isn't paying attention.
    D. Her eyelashes fall off.
5. What does April wonder about Marshall's behavior as she is being attacked?
    A. She wonders if he is safe.
    B. She wonders why he isn't calling for help.
    C. She wonders if he went back to the apartment ahead of her.
    D. She wonders if he is scared.
6. Who finally calls for help?
    A. Marshall
    B. April
    C. Melanie
    D. a strange voice
7. What happens to April's attacker?
    A. He is arrested.
    B. He runs away after someone calls for help.
    C. He puts April in his car and drives away.
    D. He surrenders to the police.

Egypt Game Multiple Choice Questions Page 25

Chapter 21:"The Hero"
1. Where do Marshall and April go after leaving Egypt?
	A. They are taken to the police station.
	B. Caroline takes them to McDonald's.
	C. They go to the drug store.
	D. They go to the airport.
2. Who is Inspector Grant?
	A. the star of Melanie's favorite television show
	B. April's father
	C. the policeman who asks the most questions about April's attack
	D. April's attacker
3. How does Marshall describe the man who grabs April?
	A. Marshall says he is a "big man,""old,"with "orange hair and spotted skin."
	B. Marshall says he looks like the Professor.
	C. Marshall says he is a young man wearing purple pants.
	D. Marshall says he did not see the man.
4. Who does Marshall identify as the man who called for help?
	A. his father
	B. Inspector Grant
	C. the janitor from the Casa Rosada
	D. the Professor
5. What does April call Caroline for the first time?
	A. Miss Caroline
	B. Mom
	C. Grandma
	D. her friend
6. Who is the man who commits the crimes?
	A. Mr. Schmitt's relative who sometimes works in his variety store
	B. the Professor
	C. a stranger from out-of-town
	D. Toby's uncle
7. How does Marshall's participation in the capture of the attacker change his behavior?
	A. He is afraid to leave the apartment alone.
	B. He no longer takes Security with him everywhere he goes.
	C. He cries all the time.
	D. Nothing changes.

Egypt Game Multiple Choice Questions Page 26

Chapter 22: "Gains and Losses"

1. What happens to the land of Egypt after April is attacked?
    A. A storm destroys it all.
    B. The parents clear everything out and throw it all away.
    C. Nothing-the gang resumes the Egypt Game immediately.
    D. It is boarded up.
2. What is the Professor's real name?
    A. Bob Tanner
    B. Captain Paulsen
    C. Dr. Huddleston
    D. Michael Townsend
3. Who begins working at the Professor's store?
    A. April
    B. Dorothea
    C. Caroline
    D. Elizabeth's mother
4. What objects does the Professor show to April?
    A. a small head of alabaster and a flat piece of marble facing from the wall of a tomb
    B. a knife and fork
    C. a quarter, a dime, and a nickel
    D. old marbles
5. To whom did these items once belong?
    A. his mother
    B. a famous archaeologist
    C. his late wife Anne
    D. King Tut
6. How does April respond to Dorothea's letter?
    A. She declines the invitation to visit Dorothea.
    B. She tells Dorothea she is ready to move back in with Dorothea and Nick.
    C. She does not respond at all.
    D. She asks Dorothea not to write to her anymore.

Egypt Game Multiple Choice Questions Page 27

Chapter 23: "Christmas Keys"
1. Who asks to see the Egypt gang on Christmas Eve?
	A. Inspector Grant
	B. the Rosses
	C. the Professor
	D. their teacher
2. What reason does the Professor give for wanting to meet with the group?
	A. He has come to tell them a story.
	B. He wants to meet all of them in person.
	C. He has nowhere else to spend the holiday.
	D. He wants to return Security.
3. What is the Professor's former profession?
	A. truck driver
	B. attorney
	C. Professor of anthropology
	D. high school principal
4. How did A-Z store get started?
	A. It began with a mail-order catalog.
	B. It began as a fund-raiser for the local high school.
	C. Mr. Ross started it as a bookstore.
	D. Anne wanted to start it in order to sell primitive handmade crafts.
5. What information does the Professor give about the oracle?
	A. He tore down the oracle after April's attack.
	B. He believes the oracle is magical.
	C. He answered Marshall's question to help him find Security.
	D. He does not mention the oracle.
6. What does the Professor give to each member of the Egypt gang?
	A. a fruitcake
	B. a key
	C. a book
	D. an artifact from his store
7. What are the Professor's plans for the future?
	A. He will begin importing, traveling, and selling goods again.
	B. He and Caroline are getting married.
	C. He is moving his home and shop to Delaware.
	D. He is going to begin teaching at the university in the fall.
8. Why does April feel sad after the children receive their keys?
	A. She will miss her friends when she moves back with Dorothea.
	B. She will miss the Professor.
	C. She fears that returning to Egypt will be a disappointment.
	D. She has lost her eyelashes.

Egypt Game Multiple Choice Questions Page 28

9. What question does April pose to Melanie at the end of the novel?
    A. "Melanie, what do you know about Gypsies?"
    B. "Melanie, will you come visit me at Dorothea's?"
    C. "Melanie, what would you like for dinner?"
    D. "Melanie, would you like to go to the playground?"

ANSWER KEY - MULTIPLE CHOICE STUDY/QUIZ QUESTIONS
The Egypt Game

Ch. 1	Ch. 2	Ch. 3	Ch. 4	Ch. 5	Ch. 6	Ch. 7	Ch. 8
1. B	1. D	1. A	1. B	1. C	1. C	1. A	1. B
2. A	2. C	2. C	2. D	2. A	2. A	2. B	2. B
3. C	3. A	3. A	3. B	3. D	3. B	3. B	3. D
4. B	4. B	4. C	4. C	4. A	4. C	4. C	4. B
5. A	5. D	5. C	5. D	5. D	5. A		5. A
6. D	6. C	6. D	6. A	6. B	6. C		6. C
	7. A	7. B		7. B	7. B		7. B
	8. C	8. D			8. A		8. B
	9. A	9. C			9. C		9. C
	10. D	10. B					

Ch. 9	Ch. 10	Ch. 11	Ch. 12	Ch. 13	Ch. 14	Ch. 15
1. A	1. B	1. C	1. A	1. C	1. A	1. A
2. A	2. C	2. C	2. A	2. C	2. B	2. B
3. B	3. D	3. B	3. C	3. A	3. D	3. C
4. C	4. B	4. D	4. B	4. C	4. B	4. B
5. C				5. B	5. C	5. B
						6. A

Ch. 16	Ch. 17	Ch. 18	Ch. 19	Ch. 20	Ch. 21	Ch. 22	Ch. 23
1. D	1. A	1. B	1. C	1. C	1. A	1. D	1. C
2. A	2. B	2. C	2. A	2. B	2. C	2. C	2. A
3. A	3. A	3. D	3. C	3. A	3. A	3. D	3. C
4. C		4. A	4. B	4. C	4. D	4. A	4. D
5. B		5. C	5. A	5. B	5. C	5. C	5. C
				6. D	6. A	6. A	6. B
				7. B	7. B		7. A
							8. C
							9. A

PREREADING VOCABULARY WORKSHEETS

VOCABULARY CHAPTERS 1-2: *The Egypt Game*

Part I: Using Prior Knowledge and Contextual Clues

Below are the sentences in which the vocabulary words appear in the text. Read the sentence. Use any clues you can find in the sentence combined with your prior knowledge, and write what you think the underlined words mean on the lines provided.

1.
A-Z
Antiques
<u>Curios</u>
Used Merchandise

_____

2. The Professor lived somewhere at the back of his <u>dingy</u> store, and when he came out to stand in the sun in his doorway, smaller children would cross the street if they had to walk by.

_____

3. Now and then, older and braver boys, inspired by the old man's strangeness, would dare each other into an attempt to tease or <u>torment</u> him–but not for long.

_____

4. . . . even for grown-ups the <u>prospect</u> of a bargain was often not enough to offset the discomfort of the old man's stony stare.

_____

5. . . . even for grown-ups the prospect of a bargain was often not enough to <u>offset</u> the discomfort of the old man's stony stare.

_____

6. He had been looking for something in a <u>seldom</u> used storeroom at the back of his shop, when a slight noise drew him to a window.

_____

7. The old man recalled that she had been in his store not long before, and along with some other improbable information she had <u>disclosed</u> that her name was April.

_____

The Egypt Game Vocabulary Worksheet Chapters 1-2 Continued

8. Diana had been moved into position near this <u>improvised</u> temple. . . .
___

9. She stood up, dumping her lap full of weeds, and reached for the blossoms–<u>gingerly</u> because of the prickles.
___

10. He also missed the <u>indignant</u> scolding when the girls discovered that April's false eyelashes had fallen before the altar of Nefertiti, where Marshall had found them. . . .
___

11. April regarded him with <u>grudging</u> admiration.
___

12. "I'm even planning to be an archaeologist when I grown up. Some people think that's a pretty kooky <u>ambition</u> for a girl–but I like it."
___

Part II: Determining the Meaning: Match the vocabulary words to their dictionary definitions.

    ____ 1. curios   A. infrequent
    ____ 2. dingy   B. strong desire to achieve something
    ____ 3. torment   C. cautiously
    ____ 4. prospect   D. compensate for
    ____ 5. offset   E. revealed
    ____ 6. seldom   F. feeling irritated by treatment one feels is unfair
    ____ 7. disclosed   G. create something from whatever is handy or available
    ____ 8. improvised   H. grimy; shabby
    ____ 9. gingerly   I. annoy or tease severely
    ____ 10. indignant   J. possibility or opportunity
    ____ 11. grudging   K. reluctance or unwillingness to give something
    ____ 12. ambition   L. a rare or interesting object

VOCABULARY CHAPTERS 3-4: *The Egypt Game*

Part I: Using Prior Knowledge and Contextual Clues

Below are the sentences in which the vocabulary words appear in the text. Read the sentence. Use any clues you can find in the sentence combined with your prior knowledge, and write what you think the underlined words mean on the lines provided.

1. . . . . she'd been brought up all over everywhere and never had much of a chance to associate with other children.

___

2. April adjusted Dorothea's old fur stole, patted up some sliding strands of hair and waited–warily.

___

3. Actually Melanie knew that April was showboating, but it occurred to her that it was probably because of homesickness.

___

4. "Reading is my favorite occupation."

___

5. April put back on her haughty face. "Of course not. Nearly everybody wears them in Hollywood."

___

6. And then the criminals escaped and were going to get revenge on Mr. Brewster.

___

7. From the Girl-Scout-cookies caper, the game moved into even more exciting escapades . . . .

___

8. Before long, with the help of a sympathetic librarian, they had found and read just about everything the library had to offer on Egypt–both fact and fiction.

___

The Egypt Game Vocabulary Worksheet Chapters 3-4 Continued

9. . . . Melanie noticed the loose plank. It had moved stiffly, that first time, with a <u>reluctant</u> rusty yelp . . . .

_____

10. April just couldn't wear those eyelashes to school on the first day. She was going to be hard enough to <u>integrate</u> even without them.

_____

11. But before the dishes were finished she had started making a <u>drastic</u> plan . . . .

_____

12. They went the wrong way first and took <u>evasive</u> action through a garage and around a stack of garbage pails.

_____

Part II: Determining the Meaning: Match the vocabulary words to their dictionary definitions.

    ____ 1. associate   A. daring adventures
    ____ 2. warily   B. acting with caution
    ____ 3. showboating   C. way to spend time
    ____ 4. occupation   D. to bring together into a whole
    ____ 5. haughty   E. seeking to avoid escape through cleverness
    ____ 6. revenge   F. be around or spend time with
    ____ 7. escapades   G. hesitant
    ____ 8. sympathetic   H. to cause harm as a "payback" for a wrong
    ____ 9. reluctant   I. having and understanding or common feeling
    ____ 10. integrate   J. arrogant; believing oneself to be superior to others
    ____ 11. drastic   K. showing–off, making reality seem grander than it is
    ____ 12. evasive   L. severe or harsh

VOCABULARY CHAPTERS 5-6: *The Egypt Game*

Part I: Using Prior Knowledge and Contextual Clues

Below are the sentences in which the vocabulary words appear in the text. Read the sentence. Use any clues you can find in the sentence combined with your prior knowledge, and write what you think the underlined words mean on the lines provided.

1. Then they scouted around and found a trash bin that was nice and roomy and not too full to hold an extra donation of dead weeds.

   _____

2. Next they turned their attention to the lean-to shed, or the Temple, as they were already beginning to call it.

   _____

3. But Melanie seemed to feel that April's short talk with the old man had made her an authority on the subject, so she was more or less obliged to come up with an opinion.

   _____

4. With one accord the girls moved warily towards the window.

   _____

5. His funny little baby-round chin was sticking out defiantly and his black eyes glared.

   _____

6. Feeling triumphant and treacherous at the same time, Melanie took the eyelashes home and hid them in her closet.

   _____

7. At last, they had to resort to making a Set themselves, from some clayey mud from the Casa Rosada's dead flower garden.

   _____

8. . . . Set's face hardened and cracked into a wicked leer, and it became clear that his strange, sunken, formless body was the very shape of evil.

   _____

The Egypt Game Vocabulary Worksheet Chapters 5-6 Continued

9. Dark and deep as the mud of the Nile, Set <u>brooded</u> lumpily...over all kinds of mystic ceremonies, weird rites and wicked plots.

_____

10. The rituals were very complicated and the correct order of processions, chants, <u>prostrations</u>, sprinklings with holy water, and sacrificial offerings had to be carefully written down . . . .

_____

Part II: Determining the Meaning: Match the vocabulary words to their dictionary definitions.

___ 1. scouted   A. untrustworthy
___ 2. lean-to   B. mutual agreement
___ 3. obliged   C. position of being stretched out on the ground
___ 4. accord   D. a building with a sloping roof that rests against the wall
                             of another, larger building
___ 5. defiantly   E. made a detailed search
___ 6. treacherous   F. to turn to out of necessity
___ 7. resort   G. an evil sidelong look
___ 8. leer   H. acting with open resistance
___ 9. brooded   I. compelled by moral force
___ 10. prostrations   J. worried over

VOCABULARY CHAPTERS 7-9: *The Egypt Game*

Part I: Using Prior Knowledge and Contextual Clues

Below are the sentences in which the vocabulary words appear in the text. Read the sentence. Use any clues you can find in the sentence combined with your prior knowledge, and write what you think the underlined words mean on the lines provided.

1. April was <u>ambushed</u> by a quick pang of sympathy, remembering how it was–missing someone and having to face a new classroom.

_____

2. "Keep a secret!" April interrupted <u>scornfully</u>. "For one thing, she's only nine years old."

_____

3. A couple of boys who were saying, "Hey, look at the new girl!" and, "Ugh! A girl!" and other typically fourth-grade remarks were suddenly silenced when they met April's <u>ferocious</u> glare.

_____

4. Elizabeth and Marshall were <u>languishing</u> in the dungeon, tied hand and foot, victims of the priests of Set.

_____

5. Even though they all <u>clamored</u> to know what was the matter, she only shook her head and said, "There's been some trouble in the neighborhood . . . ."

_____

6. There was one rumor that was particularly <u>persistent</u> and particularly troublesome to the members of the Egypt Game.

_____

7. As just about the only kid in the neighborhood who'd actually talked to the Professor, she felt she was <u>entitled</u> to have feelings about what he might do.

_____

The Egypt Game Vocabulary Worksheet Chapters 7-9 Continued

8. . . . like the fact that the Crocodile Stone seemed to have moved a tiny bit, a sure sign of its <u>sinister</u> power . . . .

_____

9. "The mighty ones have <u>summoned</u> us," Melanie chanted and dropped to her knees.

_____

10. Elizabeth had a <u>tendency</u> to worry about things like not having permission.

_____

11. "What sort of a sign?" Elizabeth wanted to know. "A secret <u>omen</u>," Melanie said.

_____

Part II: Determining the Meaning: Match the vocabulary words to their dictionary definitions.

    ____ 1. ambushed   A. a sign that predicts a future event
    ____ 2. scornfully   B. losing strength
    ____ 3. ferocious   C. called together
    ____ 4. languishing   D. with contempt
    ____ 5. clamored   E. evil
    ____ 6. persistent   F. fierce and cruel
    ____ 7. entitled   G. demanded loudly
    ____ 8. sinister   H. hit with an unexpected attack
    ____ 9. summoned   I. enduring; continuing to exist; unrelenting
    ____ 10. tendency   J. had a right to
    ____ 11. omen   K. an inclination to behave a certain way

VOCABULARY CHAPTERS 10-12: *The Egypt Game*

Part I: Using Prior Knowledge and Contextual Clues
   Below are the sentences in which the vocabulary words appear in the text. Read the sentence. Use any clues you can find in the sentence combined with your prior knowledge, and write what you think the underlined words mean on the lines provided.

1. . . . and even Mr. Kamata's sturdy real-estate-salesman's smile was beginning to wilt.

_____

2. Ken *was* sort of cute in a big blunt cocky way. He had a clean-cut all-American-Asian look about him, and he walked with a high-school swagger.

_____

3. Yeah, you little kids ought to keep up with the group better," Toby said, as he started off up the sidewalk. "You're liable to get hurt."

_____

4. By the time the Egyptians got over their convulsions of giggles, Ken and Toby had disappeared around the corner, and the lady whose walk they were on was calling to ask if they wanted some candy or not.

_____

5. "A shooting star!" Everybody repeated it in whispered unison as if they'd been rehearsed.

_____

6. April took up Melanie's theme with relish.

_____

7. Then, as the four badly shaken Egyptians turned loose of each other and tried to regain their dignity, the monster and the box-man leaned on each other and choked with fiendish laughter.

_____

8. There was no doubt about it, the enemy had faltered for a few moments, but they managed to regroup.

_____

The Egypt Game Vocabulary Worksheet Chapters 10-12 Continued

9. April <u>cringed</u>. It was such a corny, baby thing to say.

_____

10. For a few minutes the two girls <u>contemplated</u> the possibility in mournful silence.

_____

Part II: Determining the Meaning: Match the vocabulary words to their dictionary definitions.

____	1. wilt	A. wavered; hesitated
____	2. swagger	B. evil; like a fiend
____	3. liable	C. together
____	4. convulsions	D. considered; thought about intently
____	5. unison	E. likely, apt
____	6. relish	F. to droop or weaken
____	7. fiendish	G. great enjoyment
____	8. faltered	H. bent one's head and body in fear or embarrassment
____	9. cringed	I. fits of laughter
____	10. contemplated	J. to walk in an arrogant manner; strut

VOCABULARY CHAPTERS 13-15: *The Egypt Game*

Part I: Using Prior Knowledge and Contextual Clues

Below are the sentences in which the vocabulary words appear in the text. Read the sentence. Use any clues you can find in the sentence combined with your prior knowledge, and write what you think the underlined words mean on the lines provided.

1. The next day at recess Toby Alvillar <u>sidled</u> up to Melanie and April.

_____

2. "Well, obviously you've been hit by a truck and I was just wondering about the other <u>casualties</u>."

_____

3. It sat there, in the shadows among the spiderwebs, and peered down <u>balefully</u> over its tooth-scarred beak.

_____

4. As a matter of fact, he could almost do a better job of reading and writing in Egyptian than he could in English. But, since he wasn't even in kindergarten yet, he wasn't exactly <u>fluent</u> in either one.

_____

5. It was Saturday afternoon and April, Melanie, and Marshall had just come down to get Elizabeth to join the boys in Egypt for a previously scheduled <u>rendezvous</u>.

_____

6. Ken and Toby were <u>gratifyingly</u> enthusiastic.

_____

7. There the <u>bier</u> was placed on a specially prepared alter in the middle of the floor.

_____

8. At school he was Toby the cool-cat <u>sophisticate</u>; and now, suddenly, he was Toby, the grief-stricken ancient Egyptian.

_____

The Egypt Game Vocabulary Worksheet Chapters 13-15 Continued

9. And so, while Toby staggered around the alter, beating his chest with wild-eyed <u>abandon</u>, sprinkling real ashes–left over from Set's sacrificial fire–in his hair, and wailing like a wounded electric guitar . . . .

_____

10. It turned out that Queen Neferbeth felt so strongly about "cutting holes in Petey," even if he was dead, that it was decided to <u>dispense</u> with that part of the procedure.

_____

11. So the rest of the afternoon was taken up in preparing a saltwater bath for Prince Pete-ho-tep and placing him in it with the proper <u>pomp</u>.

_____

Part II: Determining the Meaning: Match the vocabulary words to their dictionary definitions.

____ 1. sidled   A. ominously; threateningly
____ 2. casualties   B. secret meeting
____ 3. balefully   C. a person who is cultured, fashionable, and refined
____ 4. fluent   D. showy display
____ 5. rendezvous   E. move sideways stealthily
____ 6. gratifyingly   F. a portable platform on which a coffin is placed prior to burial
____ 7. bier   G. able to write or speak easily
____ 8. sophisticate   H. absence of inhibitions and restraint
____ 9. abandon   I. people hurt or killed in an accident
____ 10. dispense   J. pleasingly
____ 11. pomp   K. to do without

VOCABULARY CHAPTERS 16-19: *The Egypt Game*

Part I: Using Prior Knowledge and Contextual Clues

Below are the sentences in which the vocabulary words appear in the text. Read the sentence. Use any clues you can find in the sentence combined with your prior knowledge, and write what you think the underlined words mean on the lines provided.

1. It all grew out of the fact that an assignment the class was reading just barely mentioned something called an <u>oracle</u>.

   _____

2. The oracles all had special sacred places, caves or grottoes or specially built temples, and there were all sorts of far-out things connected with them like sacred fires and mystic <u>vapors</u> and magical statues.

   _____

3. Ken was looking at April in <u>consternation</u>.

   _____

4. The other Egyptians were so caught up in his smooth <u>solemnity</u> and exalted priestly expression that they found themselves almost believing–well, half-believing–that Toby was actually talking to an ancient and powerful being. . . .

   _____

5. The other Egyptians were so caught up in his smooth solemnity and <u>exalted</u> priestly expression that they found themselves almost believing–well, half-believing–that Toby was actually talking to an ancient and powerful being . . . .

   _____

6. . . . –well, half-believing–that Toby was actually talking to an ancient and powerful being, and that something strange and <u>supernatural</u> was about to happen.

   _____

7. You know, people who were going to the oracle had to prepare themselves very carefully, so they usually shut themselves up for days without any food and <u>meditated</u> until they felt very pure and sort of dizzy . . . .

   _____

The Egypt Game Vocabulary Worksheet Chapters 16-19 Continued

8. He though and worried and thought; and at last he broke down and did something entirely against his <u>principles</u>–he called up a girl.

_____

9. "Lie to you!" Toby said. "I did not. I didn't lie once. I just gave the wrong <u>impression</u>. There's a difference."

_____

10. He reached inside, felt around for a minute, and then his face lit up with a smile so starry that for just a second the other, wiser Egyptians felt just as pleased with their oracle as he did. But after that they went right back to being <u>incredulous</u>.

_____

Part II: Determining the Meaning: Match the vocabulary words to their dictionary definitions.

____ 1. oracle   A. patches of rising moisture in the air
____ 2. vapors   B. a medium for divine prophecy
____ 3. consternation   C. anxiety
____ 4. solemnity   D. proud; glorified
____ 5. exalted   E. a formal, serious demeanor
____ 6. supernatural   F. unbelieving
____ 7. meditated   G. focus the mind on spiritual matters for an uninterrupted
                              period of time
____ 8. principles   H. a produced effect
____ 9. impression   I. rules or beliefs that govern behavior
____ 10. incredulous   J. unexplainable by the laws of nature

VOCABULARY CHAPTERS 20-23: *The Egypt Game*

Part I: Using Prior Knowledge and Contextual Clues

Below are the sentences in which the vocabulary words appear in the text. Read the sentence. Use any clues you can find in the sentence combined with your prior knowledge, and write what you think the underlined words mean on the lines provided.

1. But, as time went by, and no one burst in on them to gloat about the successful trick, that seemed less and less likely.

   _____

2. April sat there fuming for a few minutes, getting madder and madder at Ken.

   _____

3. There was something–a faint and far-away click and then a dragging shuffle–so soft as to be almost entirely lost in the distant drone of traffic and the beating of a racing heart.

   _____

4. Just then there was a commotion at the door and Inspector Grant stood up.

   _____

5. The consensus of opinion was pretty much, "That's that!" Egypt was lost and gone forever, and there was no use thinking about it.

   _____

6. It had been a place to get away to–a private lair . . . .

   _____

7. –a secret seclusion meant to be shared with best friends only–

   _____

8. They speculated about what the Professor had in mind, and had just about agreed that he was probably bringing back all their stuff . . . .

   _____

The Egypt Game Vocabulary Worksheet Chapters 20-23: Continued

9. "My subject is <u>anthropology,</u> which, as you may know, is the study of all the various kinds and conditions of . . . ."

_____

10. . . . she enrolled in a class I was teaching on <u>primitive</u> and ancient peoples because of her interest in primitive art.

_____

Part II: Determining the Meaning: Match the vocabulary words to their dictionary definitions.

___ 1. gloat   A. a constant low humming sound
___ 2. fuming   B. to show a great deal of anger
___ 3. drone   C. formed a theory without much evidence
___ 4. commotion   D. relating to man's earliest existence
___ 5. consensus   E. to smugly consider one's own success
___ 6. lair   F. study of man and his culture and religion
___ 7. seclusion   G. a state of quiet separation from others
___ 8. speculated   H. noisy confusion
___ 9. anthropology   I. general agreement
___ 10. primitive   J. a hiding place

VOCABULARY WORKSHEET ANSWER KEY
The Egypt Game

	1-2	3-4	5-6	7-9	10-12	13-15	16-19	20-23
1	L	F	E	H	F	E	B	E
2	H	B	D	D	J	I	A	B
3	I	K	I	F	E	A	C	A
4	J	C	B	B	I	G	E	H
5	D	J	H	G	C	B	D	I
6	A	H	A	I	G	J	J	J
7	E	A	F	J	B	F	G	G
8	G	I	G	E	A	C	I	C
9	C	G	J	C	H	H	H	F
10	F	D	C	K	D	K	F	D
11	K	L		A		D		
12	B	E						

DAILY LESSONS

LESSON ONE

Objectives
1. To introduce the process of rule-making and compromise
2. To distribute the books and other materials necessary for the unit
3. To preview the novel by drawing conclusions from the cover and table of contents

Activity #1

Before students come into the classroom, arrange the desks into groups of 5 or 6. Allow students to sit where they like, as long as they do not disturb the pre-arranged groupings. After all students are seated, give each group a game board and a set of 20 playing pieces-10 each of two different styles (these might be 10 pennies and 10 dimes, different colors of checkers, etc). You may also choose to give students one die per group. *A copy of the game board is included at the end of this lesson. Make as many copies as necessary for your class. You may choose to laminate the game boards to provide extra durability.* Without any further instructions, give your class ten or fifteen minutes to "play the game." Be sure to walk around the classroom to maintain order, but do not answer any questions about how the game itself should be played. Ask each group to record any rules or order for play as they develop.

(Note to teacher: If time permits, or if you would like to continue with this activity, you may have groups trade their instructions with one another. Ask the students to play according to the new set of rules. Afterwards, ask groups whether the instructions from the other group were clear enough to play the game from beginning to end. What improvements or changes would the second group make? The class may even decide to develop a master set of rules for the game, refining the ideas from the entire class. Another class could then swap rules for play.)

This game is actually based on the ancient Egyptian game of Senet, which you may or may not want to share with your class. Students may research the game further throughout this unit if time permits. If you choose to research the game, you will discover a great deal of ambiguity regarding the details of how it was played.

Activity #2

After each group has recorded its rules, ask one member of each group to read the rules aloud to the class. You may ask another student to record the collective rules on the board or overhead projector, noting any similarities and highlighting differences.

Following the group reports, discuss the process with the class. The following questions may serve as a guide:

How did you feel when I first told you to "use the game boards and tokens to play any way that you like?" Were you intimidated? Excited? Disinterested?

Did the game become more challenging or less challenging without an established set of rules to guide you?

Was your group able to come to an agreement regarding the way the game would be played? If so, how did you resolve differences of opinion to reach the common goal? If not, what were the biggest obstacles?

Were you able to clearly define the rules of play in your group?

TRANSITION: "In the Zilpha Keatley Snyder's novel *The Egypt Game,* we are going to read about a group of students who build friendships through their participation in a game with no set rules, not unlike the experience you had today. For the remainder of this unit, the groups that you formed today will be known as your 'Egypt Group.' Whenever we work in groups, you will work with the Egypt Group that you established today."

Activity #3

Distribute the materials students will use in this unit. Explain in detail how students are to use these materials.

Study Guides Students should read the study guide questions for each reading assignment prior to beginning the reading assignment to get a feeling for what events and ideas are important in the section they are about to read. After reading the section, students will (as a class or individually) answer the questions to review the important events and ideas from that section of the book. Students should keep the study guides as study materials for the unit test.

Vocabulary Prior to reading a reading assignment, students will do vocabulary work related to the section of the book they are about to read. Following the completion of the reading of the book, there will be a vocabulary review of all the words used in the vocabulary assignments. Students should keep their vocabulary work as study materials for the unit test.

Reading Assignment Sheet You need to fill in the reading assignment sheet to let students know by when their reading has to be completed. You can either write the assignment sheet up on a side blackboard or bulletin board and leave it there for students to see each day, or you can "ditto" copies for each student to have. In either case, you should advise students to become very familiar with the reading assignments so they know what is expected of them.

Extra Activities Center The Unit Resource Materials portion of this LitPlan contains suggestions for an extra library of related books and articles in your classroom as well as crossword and word search puzzles. Make an extra activities center in your room where you will keep these materials for students to use. (Bring the books and articles in from the library and keep several copies of the puzzles on hand.) Explain to students that these materials are available for students to use when they finish reading assignments or other class work early.

Nonfiction Assignment Sheet Explain to students that they each are to read at least one non-fiction piece from the in-class library at some time during the unit. Students will fill out a nonfiction assignment sheet after completing the reading to help you (the teacher) evaluate their reading experiences and to help the students think about and evaluate their own reading experiences.

Books Each school has its own rules and regulations regarding student use of school books. Advise students of the procedures that are normal for your school. Preview the book. Look at the covers, front-matter, and index. Glance through at some of the drawings.

<u>Activity #4</u>
Give students the opportunity to look at the book cover, table of contents, and illustrations with their group members from Activity #1. As a class, discuss: "what do you think this book will be about? What are your predictions about *The Egypt Game*? You may decide to post responses on individual paper strips on the bulletin board, or you may use the topic as a prompt for a journal entry.

GAME BOARD

1	20	21
2	19	22
3	18	23
4	17	24
5	16	25
6	15	26
7	14	27
8	13	28
9	12	29
10	11	30

NONFICTION ASSIGNMENT SHEET - *The Egypt Game*
(To be completed after reading the required nonfiction article)

Name _____ Date _____

Title of Nonfiction Read _____

Written By _____ Publication Date _____

I. Factual Summary: Write a short summary of the piece you read.

II. Vocabulary
    1. With which vocabulary words in the piece did you encounter some degree of difficulty?

    2. How did you resolve your lack of understanding with these words?

III. Interpretation: What was the main point the author wanted you to get from reading his work?

IV. Criticism
    1. With which points of the piece did you agree or find easy to accept? Why?

    2. With which points of the piece did you disagree or find difficult to believe? Why?

V. Personal Response: What do you think about this piece? <u>OR</u> How does this piece influence your ideas?

LESSON TWO

Objectives
    1. To familiarize students with the study guide questions for chapters 1-2
    2. To familiarize students with vocabulary for chapters 1-2
    3. To read chapters 1-2 ("The Discovery of Egypt" and "Enter April")
    4. To give students practice reading orally
    5. To evaluate students' oral reading

Activity #1
    Students should read over the study guide questions for the first two chapters of the novel in order to get a feel for the reading assignment. Next, have students complete the vocabulary worksheet for chapters 1-2.

Activity #2
    Have students read chapters 1 and 2 of *The Egypt Game* aloud in class. You probably know the best way to select readers in your classroom; pick students at random, ask for volunteers, or use whatever method works best for your group. If you have not yet completed an oral reading evaluation for your students this period, this would be a good opportunity to do so. A form is included with this unit for your convenience.

Activity #3 (Homework, if time does not permit in class)
    Give students a few minutes to formulate answers for the study guide questions for Chapters 1 and 2. Discuss the answers to the questions in Lesson Three.

ORAL READING EVALUATION *The Egypt Game*

Name _____ Class____ Date _____

SKILL	EXCELLENT	GOOD	AVERAGE	FAIR	POOR
Fluency	5	4	3	2	1
Clarity	5	4	3	2	1
Audibility	5	4	3	2	1
Pronunciation	5	4	3	2	1
_____	5	4	3	2	1
_____	5	4	3	2	1

Total _____   Grade _____

Comments:

LESSON THREE

Objectives
1. To discuss the answers to the study questions for chapters 1-2
2. To familiarize students with the study guide questions for chapters 3-4
3. To familiarize students with vocabulary for chapters 3-4
4. To read chapters 3-4 ("Enter Melanie–and Marshall" and "The Egypt Girls")
5. To give students practice reading orally
6. To evaluate students' oral reading

Activity #1

Students were to formulate answers for the study questions for chapters 1-2 as homework. Take a few minutes at the beginning of this class to discuss the answers to those questions in detail. Write the answers on the board or overhead transparency so students can have the correct answers for study purposes.

Note: It is a good practice in public speaking and leadership skills for individual students to take charge of leading the discussions of the study questions. Perhaps a different student could go to the front of the class and lead the discussion each day that the study questions are discussed during this unit. Of course, the teacher should guide the discussion when appropriate and be sure to fill in any gaps the students leave.

Activity #2

Give students about 15 minutes to preview the study guide questions and complete the vocabulary worksheet for chapters 3-4.

Activity #3

Have students read chapters 3-4 aloud in class. If you have not yet completed an oral reading evaluation for your students this period, this would be a good opportunity to do so.

LESSON FOUR

Objectives
1. To review the main events and ideas from chapters 3-4
2. To familiarize students with the study guide questions for chapters 5-6
3. To familiarize students with vocabulary for chapters 5-6
4. To read chapters 5-6 ("The Evil God and the Secret Spy" and "Eyelashes and Ceremony")
5. To give students practice reading orally
6. To evaluate students' oral reading

Activity #1
Have students formulate answers to the study guide questions for chapters 3-4. You may assign certain questions to individuals or small groups, or you may answer the questions as a class. Take time to discuss the answers to the questions in detail.

Activity #2
Give students about 15 minutes to preview the study guide questions and complete the vocabulary worksheet for chapters 5-6.

Activity #3
Have students read chapters 5-6 aloud in class. If you have not yet completed an oral reading evaluation for your students this period, this would be a good opportunity to do so.

LESSON FIVE

Objectives
1. To review the main ideas and events from chapters 5-6
2. To familiarize students with the study guide questions for chapters 7-9
3. To familiarize students with vocabulary for chapters 7-9
4. To read chapters 7-9 ("Neferbeth," "Prisoners of Fear," and "Summoned by the Mighty Ones")
5. To give students practice reading orally
6. To evaluate students' oral reading

Activity #1
Have students formulate answers to the study guide questions for chapters 5-6. You may assign certain questions to individuals or small groups, or you may answer the questions as a class. Take time to discuss the answers to the questions in detail.

Activity #2
Give students about 15 minutes to preview the study guide questions and complete the vocabulary worksheet for chapters 7-9.

Activity #3
Have students read chapters 7-9 aloud in class. If you have not yet completed an oral reading evaluation for your students this period, this would be a good opportunity to do so. If you have completed the oral reading evaluations, students may read silently.

Activity #3 (Homework if time does not permit in class)
Have students write answers to the study guide questions for chapters 7-9. Students should have the questions completed by the next class meeting.

*Remind students that there will be a quiz over the study questions for chapters 1-9 at the next class meeting.

LESSON SIX

Objectives
1. To quiz students on the study guide questions for chapters 1-9
2. To familiarize students with the study guide questions for chapters 10-12
3. To familiarize students with vocabulary for chapters 10-12
4. To read chapters 10-12 ("The Return to Egypt," "Egypt Invaded," and "Elizabethan Diplomacy")

Activity #1
Quiz - Distribute quizzes and give students about 10 minutes to complete them. Be sure to include all the study questions for chapters 7-9 because you have not discussed all of them in class; just be sure students are aware of the correct answers to study from for the unit test.

(Note: You may use the multiple choice version of the study questions for this quiz, or you may choose to read a selection of short answer study guide questions aloud instead. Have students exchange papers. Grade the quizzes as a class. Collect the papers for recording the grades. If you used the multiple choice version as a quiz, take a few minutes to discuss the answers for the short answer version if your students are using the short answer version for their study guides.)

Activity #2
Give students about 15 minutes to preview the study guide questions and complete the vocabulary worksheet for chapters 10-12.

Activity #3
Have students begin reading chapters 10-12.

> *Note: To vary the week's plan, you may decide–for any of the lessons–to give students an opportunity to read the novel silently, rather than orally, or to assign some of the reading for homework. You may also choose to break up the many days of reading with some of the extra activities found in the Unit Resource Materials. Some teachers have had students read to each other in small groups or have read orally assigning character "parts" to various students.*

Activity #4 (Homework if time does not permit in class)
Have students formulate answers to the study guide questions for chapters 10-12.

LESSONS SEVEN AND EIGHT

Objectives
1. To review the main ideas and events from chapters 10-12
2. To give students an opportunity to practice interpersonal skills in a small group
3. To familiarize students with the study guide questions for chapters 13-19
4. To familiarize students with vocabulary for chapters 13-19
5. To read chapters 13-19 ("Moods and Maybes," "Hieroglyphics," "The Ceremony for the Dead," "The Oracle of Thoth," "The Oracle Speaks," "Where is Security?" "Confession and Confusion")
6. To give students the opportunity to develop their own plan of study for the novel

Activity #1
   Have students formulate answers to the study guide questions for chapters 10-12. You may assign certain questions to individuals or small groups, or you may answer the questions as a class. Take time to discuss the answers to the questions in detail.

Activity #2
Note: Essentially, students will be completing the same work for chapters 13-19 as they did for the previous twelve chapters; however, they will be reading and studying chapters 13-19 in their Egypt Groups in order to mimic the cohesion of the Egypt group in the novel and provide a real-life connection to the characters' experiences (while also easing the possible monotony of daily oral reading). You may need to alter this approach, depending on your own class needs.

Divide students into their "Egypt groups." Explain to them that over the next two days, they will be responsible for previewing the study guide questions for chapters 13-19, completing the vocabulary worksheets for chapters 13-19, reading chapters 13-19, and answering the study guide questions for chapters 13-19. Each group will determine how to accomplish these tasks, what each group member's responsibility will be, which work will be completed in class, and how reading assignments will be completed. All of the work must be finished by the beginning of class on Lesson 9. Circulate through the classroom and talk with individual groups over the next two days to maintain order and clarify any points of confusion the students may have throughout the group study. This is also a good time to discuss the novel with smaller numbers of students and get their reactions to the text.

Note: Depending on the level of your students, you might need to check the groups' plans and approve them before students continue into the work.

Activity #2
   Group work on chapters 13-19

*You may choose to quiz students on these chapters in Lesson Nine using the multiple choice study guide questions.

LESSON NINE

Objectives
1. To review the main events and ideas from chapters 13-19
2. To familiarize students with the study guide questions for chapters 20-23
3. To familiarize students with vocabulary for chapters 20-23
4. To read chapters 20-23 ("Fear Strikes," "The Hero," "Gains and Losses," and "Christmas Keys")

Activity #1
    Distribute the multiple choice study questions for chapters 13-15 and 16-19 as quizzes on these sections to help evaluate students' group work. After students complete the quizzes, discuss the answers in detail as a class.

Activity #2
Students should preview the study questions, do the vocabulary work and read chapters 20-23 during this class period. Any work not completed by the end of the class should be done prior to the next class meeting.

LESSON TEN

Objectives
    1. To review the study guide questions for chapters 20-23
    2. To explain the requirements for the group project
    3. To make topic assignments for the group project

Activity #1
    Discuss the answers to the study questions for chapters 20-23. This may also be a good time for students to ask any other questions about the factual aspects of the novel that might confuse them.

Activity #2
    Students will break into their Egypt groups to begin working on the class project. (You may either allow groups to choose their own topics for research, or you may assign a topic to each group–you know which method will be better for your students). A selection of possible topics is listed below. You may choose to list these on the board in order for the class to brainstorm additional topics before making the final choices/assignments. Each of the following topics is referred to in *The Egypt Game*:

        Hieroglyphics
        Mummies and mummification
        Tombs/Pyramids
        Pharaohs (general and specific)
        Priestesses (general and specific)
        Egyptian dress/costuming
        Oracles
        Ceremonies
        Legends/Riddles/Curses

    After each group has chosen (or been assigned) a topic, discuss the requirements for the project, as well as the grading system, which you will determine according to the needs of your class or the specific nature of your course. A library research day is scheduled for Lesson 13, and group presentations are scheduled for Lesson 20. Of course, these can be scheduled any day that best suits your class schedule. In general, each group should present a paper, as well as a product (i.e. video, system of hieroglyphics, sculpture) for their final project.

LESSON ELEVEN

Objectives
1. To give students practice expressing their personal opinions about the novel
2. To give students practice analyzing internal and external conflicts
3. To give students practice writing in an alternate form
4. To give students an opportunity to analyze character thoughts and motivations
5. To give the teacher an opportunity to evaluate student writing

Activity

Distribute Writing Assignment #1. Discuss the directions in detail and give students ample time to complete the assignment. Collect the papers at the end of the class period.

Follow-up

After you have graded the assignments, have a writing conference with the students (This unit schedules one in Lesson 13). After the writing conference, allow students to revise their papers using your suggestions and corrections. Give them about three days from the date they receive their papers to complete the revision. I suggest grading the revisions on an A-C-E scale (all revisions well-done, some revisions made, few or no revisions made). This will speed your grading time and still give some credit for the students' efforts.

WRITING ASSIGNMENT #1 - *The Egypt Game*

PROMPT
Throughout the novel, the characters struggle with internal and external conflicts. Choose one of the characters from the novel and write a diary entry in which you, as the character, describe an external conflict (a struggle with a person or force outside himself or herself) or internal conflict (a struggle within one's self, such as a battle with one's conscience) evident in the novel.

PREWRITING
Brainstorm conflicts that occur in the novel. You may choose to make two lists: Internal and External. From those lists, determine whether one character appeals to you more than others. Did you feel a connection with one of the characters? Could you relate to a conflict evident in the novel? Would you like to write from the point of view of a character with whom you did *not* feel a connection (this might help you understand that character a little better). You may even choose to write from the point of view of a minor character in the novel.

DRAFTING
Since this is a diary entry, the style may be less formal than a speech or essay. The entry is a personal record of the character's thoughts, so you may adopt a more conversational tone. You will also want to capture the style of the character you are portraying. Certainly the writing and language in the Professor's entry would differ greatly from Marshall's composition.

You should still have an opening paragraph that identifies the conflict and states whether it is a struggle with someone else or strictly within yourself.

Two or three paragraphs should follow the introduction that describe how the conflict arose, the effects the conflict is having on you and those around you, possible resolutions to the conflict, and any obstacles to that resolution.

In a concluding paragraph, outline how you intend to resolve the conflict, or if you foresee a resolution at all.

PROMPT
When you finish the rough draft of your composition, ask a student who sits near you to read it. After reading your rough draft, he/she should tell you what he/she liked best about your work, which parts were difficult to understand, and ways in which your work could be improved. Reread your paper considering your critic's comments, and make the corrections you think are necessary. Ask your classmate what he/she thought of each of the characters/events you chose for your assignment.

PROOFREADING
Do a final proofreading of your paper double-checking your grammar, spelling, organization, and the clarity of your ideas.

WRITING EVALUATION FORM - *The Egypt Game*

Name _____ Date _____

Grade _____

Circle One For Each Item:

Grammar:	correct	errors noted on paper
Spelling:	correct	errors noted on paper
Punctuation:	correct	errors noted on paper
Legibility:	excellent	good fair poor
_____	excellent	good fair poor
_____	excellent	good fair poor

Strengths:

Weaknesses:

Comments/Suggestions:

LESSON TWELVE

Objective
> To review all of the vocabulary work done in this unit

Activity 1
> Choose one (or more) of the vocabulary review activities listed below and spend your class period as directed in the activity. Some of the materials for these review activities are located in the Vocabulary Resource Materials section in this LitPlan.

VOCABULARY REVIEW ACTIVITIES

1. Divide your class into two teams and have an old-fashioned spelling or definition bee.

2. Give each of your students (or students in groups of two, three or four) an *The Egypt Game* Vocabulary Word Search Puzzle. The person (group) to find all of the vocabulary words in the puzzle first wins.

3. Give students an *The Egypt Game* Vocabulary Word Search Puzzle without the word list. The person or group to find the most vocabulary words in the puzzle wins.

4. Use an *The Egypt Game* Vocabulary Crossword Puzzle. Put the puzzle onto a transparency on the overhead projector (so everyone can see it), and do the puzzle together as a class.

5. Give students an *The Egypt Game* Vocabulary Matching Worksheet to do.

6. Divide your class into two teams. Use *The Egypt Game* vocabulary words with their letters jumbled as a word list. Student 1 from Team A faces off against Student 1 from Team B. You write the first jumbled word on the board. The first student (1A or 1B) to unscramble the word wins the chance for his/her team to score points. If 1A wins the jumble, go to student 2A and give him/her a definition. He/she must give you the correct spelling of the vocabulary word which fits that definition. If he/she does, Team A scores a point, and you give student 3A a definition for which you expect a correctly spelled matching vocabulary word. Continue giving Team A definitions until some team member makes an incorrect response. An incorrect response sends the game back to the jumbled-word face off, this time with students 2A and 2B. Instead of repeating giving definitions to the first few students of each team, continue with the student after the one who gave the last incorrect response on the team. For example, if Team B wins the jumbled-word face-off, and student 5B gave the last incorrect answer for Team B, you would start this round of definition questions with student 6B, and so on. The team with the most points wins!

7. Have students write a story in which they correctly use as many vocabulary words as possible. Have students read their compositions orally! Post the most original compositions on your bulletin board!

LESSON THIRTEEN

Objectives
1. To allow students time to research their Egypt Group topic
2. To broaden students knowledge about ancient Egypt
3. To give students experience using various research methods
4. To discuss/evaluate students' previous writing assignment
5. To give students experience working in a group

Activity

Take students to the library/media center to find articles, books, etc. about their Egypt Group assignment (see Lesson Ten). Each group should use a minimum of three sources in their research. Suggest that students begin by dividing their responsibilities. For example, one member might be responsible for searching on the computer while another may look through books pertaining to the subject. Other members may brainstorm sub-topics related to their main topic. Since the process of working in a group and establishing a group dynamic is as important to understanding this particular novel as the final product the group produces, allow students to explore and establish their own guidelines whenever feasible.

While students are working, circulate to answer questions and conduct individual writing conferences with students regarding Writing Assignment 1.

LESSON FOURTEEN

Objectives
1. To discuss the novel on a deeper than direct recall level
2. To focus on interpretation, critical analysis, and personal response

Activity #1

Choose the questions from the Extra Discussion Questions/Writing Assignments which seem most appropriate for your students. A class discussion of these questions is most effective if students have been given the opportunity to formulate answers to the questions prior to the discussion. To this end, you may either have all the students formulate answers to all the questions, divide your class into groups and assign one or more questions to each group, or you could assign one question to each student in your class. The option you choose will make a difference in the amount of class time needed for this activity. The class discussion of these questions is scheduled for the second portion of the class, but could take place on a later day if you would like to give your students more time to prepare their answers.

NOTE: The use of graphic organizers may be helpful to students in preparing their answers. Encourage them to use any diagrams or graphics that they feel are necessary.

Activity #2

Class discussion of the Extra Discussion Questions/Writing Assignments

EXTRA WRITING ASSIGNMENTS/DISCUSSION QUESTIONS - *The Egypt Game*

Interpretation

1. From what point of view is the story told, and why is that important?

2. Is the story of *The Egypt Game* believable? Why or why not? Does it matter?

3. Are the characters in *The Egypt Game* stereotypes? If so, explain the usefulness of employing stereotypes in the book. If they are not, explain how they merit individuality.

4. What are the main conflicts in the story, and how are they resolved?

5. Describe the author's writing style.

6. *The Egypt Game* is a very short novel. Could anything have been gained by including more scenes from the time before or after the events of the story? If so, what could have been added and for what purpose? If not, explain why not.

7. Plot the rise and fall of action in *The Egypt Game*.

Critical

1. How do April's experiences in the novel change her relationship with Dorothea? Give examples.

2. How does April's relationship with Caroline change throughout the novel? What events bring about these changes?

3. How did Marshall know that the Professor had been watching them, though no one else did?

4. How does the Professor influence the Egypt Game throughout the novel?

5. What roles do the parents and guardians play in this novel? Compare and contrast the different parents in the novel and note how they influence their children.

6. Why are the eyelashes important at the beginning of the novel? What do they tell us about April?

7. What do the eyelashes symbolize?

8. Compare and contrast April and Melanie.

9. Compare and contrast Toby and Ken.

Egypt Game Extra Discussion Questions/Writing Assignments Page 2

10. Why didn't Marshall tell the other members of the Egypt group that someone was watching them?

11. Compare and contrast Schmitt's Variety Store and A-Z.

12. What causes Toby to confess his actions about the oracle to Melanie and April?

13. Compare April's and Toby's family life. How are they different? How are they alike?

14. What does Egypt become to each of the characters?

15. What are the major conflicts in the novel? Consider both internal and external conflicts.

16. Compare and contrast the Professor with Mr. Schmitt. Include information about their stores in your discussion.

Critical/Personal Response
1. How do the "rules" and "procedures" of the Egypt Game change as each new player is added? Do you think the game improves as the group expands?

2. How is this a "game" in the traditional sense? How is it different?

3. In what ways might the Professor be a Security for the Egypt gang? How so?

4. Do you think the Egypt gang would have become friends if it weren't for their common interest in Egypt? Cite examples from the novel.

Personal Response
1. Do you know of a shop like the A-Z? Where is it? Do you agree with April that "old things" are more interesting?

2. Did you have a "Security" of your own as a child? What was it? Do you remember when you began letting go of the item? How did it feel? Do you still have the item?

3. The players decide to break from the game for a while until they can raise money to buy colored pens. Have there been times in your life when you raised money to purchase an item or give to a cause? Was it worth the time and effort? What inspired you to undertake the activity?

Egypt Game Extra Discussion Questions/Writing Assignments Page 3

4. The Egypt gang relied heavily upon artifacts and research in their efforts to reproduce an authentic Egypt on Orchard Avenue. What items from today's time might be considered artifacts centuries from now? How might they be interpreted– or misinterpreted--by future generations?

5. What ceremonies exist in our culture? List and explain religious and non-religious examples.

6. Who is your favorite character? Why? Find a passage from the novel that contains a description of your character or that demonstrates a quality that you admire.

7. With whom (from the novel) would you most like to be friends?

8. With whom did you most identify?

9. What questions do you still have about the novel?

Quotations

1. And one of the things they had in common, at that time, was a vague and mysterious fear of the old man called the Professor.

2. He didn't talk very much, but when he did he always said exactly what he wanted to without any trouble.

3. You never could tell with kids–they didn't do things in a pattern, the way grown-ups did.

4. There was only one thing that April didn't seem to know much about–that was getting along with people.

5. But even without the eyelashes Melanie had a hard time trying to translate April into something that Wilson School could understand and appreciate.

6. So when they started calling April, February, Melanie knew that everything would be all right.

7. And there was something about the carved perfection of her face that made her smile seem like magic–an enchanted ivory princess warming suddenly to life.

8. She'd noticed before that April, in spite of her sophisticated ways, really didn't know much at all about certain kinds of things. The kinds of things parents tell their children when they're alone together and other kids tell you if they know you really well. All April's information seemed to be the kind of things grown-ups let you overhear, and of course, nearly everything she could find in the children's part of libraries.

Egypt Game Extra Discussion Questions/Writing Assignments Page 4

9. Both the bigger girls looked surprised. Elizabeth wasn't the kind of person you expect to come up with ideas in an emergency.

10. But Toby shook his head. "I don't feel like playing basketball," he said. "Besides, I sort of go for this Egypt stuff. Let's hang around awhile. Okay?"

11. "After all," Toby said, "Thoth was the Egyptian god of wisdom, and this crazy priestess bit was something the Greeks thought up."

12. "Lie to you!" Toby said. "I did not. I didn't lie to you once. I just gave the wrong impression. There's a difference."

13. "Well," April and Melanie said to each other–only just with a look, not out loud, "wasn't that like a boy. They got things into a mess and then expected a girl to get them out of it."

14. Marshall for some reason had turned around and was aiming the light in the opposite direction, on the wall of the Professor's store, but at her whisper he turned back.

15. He said Security didn't want his picture taken. After that he started leaving Security home sometimes when he went places, and before too long, he didn't need to have Security with him at all anymore, excepting to hold on to at night when he was sleepy.

16. It had been a place to get away to–a private lair–a secret seclusion meant to be shared with best friends only–a life unknown to grown-ups and lived by kids alone."

17. And contact–involvement–was what I had spent years eliminating entirely from my life.

18. I stood there holding the block of wood in my hand, and then Marshall turned around and looked at me. I could see that he knew that I was there and that he was asking me to help. And then I broke the glass–

19. Yeah, and it's just awful when you go back to something that was so great the way you remembered it and it's no good anymore. It even ruins remembering.

LESSON FIFTEEN

Objectives
1. To widen the breadth of students' knowledge about the topics discussed or touched upon in *The Egypt Game*
2. To check students' nonfiction reading assignments
3. To give students practice public speaking

Activity #1

Ask each student to give a brief oral report about the nonfiction articles he/she read for the unit project assignment. Your criteria for evaluating this report will vary depending on the level of your students. You may wish for students to give a complete report without using notes of any kind, or you may want students to read directly from a written report, or you may want to do something in between these two extremes. Just make students aware of your criteria in ample time for them to prepare their reports.

Start with one student's report. After that, ask if anyone else in the class has read on a topic related to the first student's report. If no one has, choose another student at random. After each report, be sure to ask if anyone has a report related to the one just completed. That will help keep a continuity during the discussion of the reports. After all reports on a topic are given, take a minute to hold a short class discussion about the information students have just heard.

Activity #2

If time remains after the reports are completed, you may choose to give students class time to work on their group presentations, or work on another activity provided with this unit.

*Remind students to bring in a newspaper article for the next class period (Journalism study).

LESSON SIXTEEN

Objectives
1. To introduce students to newspaper writing
2. To have students analyze a newspaper article to determine objectivity

Activity #1
Have each student bring a newspaper article to class. Have some additional articles available from a variety of newspaper sources.

First, have students write down the headlines from their articles to share with the class. What do they think each article will be about? What drew them to this particular article?

Individually or in small groups, ask students to peruse their articles and jot down all the *facts* they find. Where does the writer claim he got the facts? Does he cite (or name) his sources in the article? Ask students why they believe that it is important for the writer to sometimes cite his sources. Do the students feel the information contained in the article is reliable? Why or why not?

Compare and contrast two articles about a similar subject from two different newspapers. What is the date on each article? Is it clear which article was written first by the content? What skills must a successful newspaper reporter possess?

Activity #2
Have your school newspaper available (if your school has one). What information does it contain? What heros does it highlight?

Note: You may decide to begin printing a newsletter with your class, monthly, weekly, or unit-by-unit. Ask students what columns should be contained in each newsletter.

LESSON SEVENTEEN

Objectives
1. To give the teacher an opportunity to evaluate student writing
2. To give students practice writing a factual article
3. To give students practice writing in a journalistic style
4. To give students an opportunity to analyze and interpret facts in the novel

Activity
Distribute Writing Assignment #2. Discuss the directions in detail and give students ample time to complete the assignment.

WRITING ASSIGNMENT #2 - *The Egypt Game*

PROMPT
In the chapter entitled "The Hero," Snyder writes:

> The next day it was all in the papers. The red-headed man had admitted everything.... April's picture was in the paper and so was Marshall's. There was a long story about how Marshall had saved the Professor from being unjustly accused and described the murderer so that the police were able to catch him. But April and Melanie were a little bit disgusted with the way the reporter talked about Marshall's description.

Write the article that appears in the newspaper mentioned above. Be sure to remain consistent with any facts that are presented in the novel, but also fill in any additional details to compose your narrative. Consider the techniques that we examined during our journalism lesson. DON'T FORGET TO WRITE A HEADLINE FOR YOUR ARTICLE

PREWRITING
Begin by rereading sections of the novel that pertain to this article. What elements are missing that you might wish to include? Make a list of any irrefutable evidence that you come across.

DRAFTING
Consider our previous study of journalism and the newspaper articles we read in class. The writing for articles is generally concise, informative, and to the point.

Begin your article with an introductory paragraph, which should introduce the story, and history of the story, to the reader. Follow the initial paragraph with an explanation of the facts surrounding the crimes committed in the community, the crime committed against April, the investigation which led to the close of the cases, and the major players involved in each phase of the story.

Conclude the article by relating the status of the case today.

PROMPT
When you finish the rough draft of your paper, ask a student who sits near you to read it. After reading your rough draft, he/she should tell you what he/she liked best about your work, which parts were difficult to understand, and ways in which your work could be improved. Reread your paper considering your critic's comments, and make the corrections you think are necessary.

PROOFREADING
Do a final proofreading of your paper double-checking your grammar, spelling, organization, and the clarity of your ideas.

LESSON EIGHTEEN

Objectives
1. To define the terms diction, imagery, personification, and mood
2. To demonstrate how Snyder's use of language contributes to the mood of the work
3. To allow students to explore the development of imagery and mood in their original work

Activity #1

Write the words "diction," "personification," "imagery," and "mood" on the board. Ask students if they know what these words mean. If they need prompting, ask them to examine the words closely for similarities to other words that they know ("dictionary," "person," "image," "good mood/bad mood").

Explain to students that these four terms are interrelated when crafting writing and language.

> Diction- word choice
> Personification- the assignment of human qualities to a non-human thing
> Imagery-figurative language or a collection of visual images
> Mood- the feeling or atmosphere created in a work of literature

(A passage from "Fear Strikes"--Chapter 20--is used as an example for this lesson. There are many others throughout the novel that could work equally as well).

Read the following passage aloud to your students:

> It was very quiet and very dark in the alley and familiar things loomed up suddenly, huge and out of shape. The flashlight beam, none too steady in April's hand, made trash bins crouch and garbage pails lurk, and a length of hose slither against a wall. Imagination is a great thing in long dull hours, but it's a real curse in a dark alley, and April's imagination had always been out of the ordinary. She would have hated to admit it, but right at that moment, even a four-year-old was a little bit comforting...Especially a four-year-old who could march steadfastly by a garbage can that had suddenly developed a hunchback and great lopsided eyes, without even seeming to notice.

After reading the passage, asks students to use one word to describe how the scene *feels*. Brainstorm these responses (this is the mood of the piece). Next ask students what elements work together to create that feeling (diction, imagery, and personification). List words on the bored as the students identify them. Identify personification within this passage and explain what makes it personification.

Activity #2

Individually, in small groups, or as a class, find other excerpts from the novel that demonstrate strong use of figurative language. Give students an opportunity to explain why they made the choices that they did.
How would the mood of the novel change if the descriptive passages and figurative language were dulled?

Activity #3 (May be completed for homework if time does not permit)
Give students an option for this assignment. Option #1: Students may illustrate the passage from Activity #1. In addition, ask them to write a paragraph or two that describes how Snyder's language, imagery, diction, and figurative language guided their own illustrations. Option #2: Students may compose an original paragraph of descriptive or narrative writing. In addition, ask them to write a paragraph or two that explains why they used the language that they chose. How might the passage be altered if the language were altered? Allow class time for students to share their work with one another.

LESSON NINETEEN

Objectives
    1. To give students the opportunity to practice writing to persuade
    2. To encourage students' critical thinking skills
    3. To have students explore a real-life connection to *The Egypt Game*
    4. To give the teacher the opportunity to evaluate students' writing skills

Activity
    Distribute Writing Assignment #3. Discuss the directions in detail and give students ample time to complete the assignment. While students are writing, call individual students to your desk or some other private area for a writing conference based on the first two writing assignments in this unit. An evaluation form is included in this unit for your convenience.

WRITING ASSIGNMENT #3 - *The Egypt Game*

PROMPT

Throughout the novel *The Egypt Game*, the characters use various methods to effect change in their community and their world. For instance, Snyder alludes to the peace and freedom demonstrations of the 1960s, while Mr. Schmitt attempts to use letter-writing and community petitions to "invite" the Professor to leave the community.

Identify a change that you believe should be made in your school or community.

Why should such change be effected? What method or methods would you employ to accomplish your goal? Identify a major obstacle you might face before reaching your goal and suggest how you might overcome that obstacle.

PREWRITING

You might begin by brainstorming changes you would like to make in the world around you. You might divide your list into categories, such as "school" or "community." Select one item from this list to address in your essay.

You will also need to consider arguments to your proposal. Why might people want to keep things the way they are? What are the drawbacks to the changes that you are proposing? Why is the current system inferior to the one you are proposing?

After choosing your topic, list reasons why you believe this change should be made. Would it improve the lives of others? How? What difficulties exist now that would be solved by the changes you are proposing?

How will you achieve your goal? What methods will you use to educate and convince others that your change will be an improvement over the current way of doing things?

DRAFTING

Write an introductory paragraph that highlights the topic you will discuss. Why is this change necessary, how will you make it, and what improvements will result? In the next paragraph, explain your reasons in more depth. Point out why other people might disagree with you, and then explain why your opposition is wrong. Next, write a paragraph outlining your plan to get your change accomplished. Be sure to explain how any time, effort, or money required to accomplish your goal is well worth the cost. Conclude by describing your school or community AFTER the improvement has been made.

PROMPT

When you finish the rough draft of your paper, ask a student who sits near you to read it. After reading your rough draft, he/she should tell you what he/she liked best about your work, which parts were difficult to understand, and ways in which your work could be improved. Reread your paper considering your critic's comments, and make the corrections you think are necessary.

PROOFREADING

Do a final proofreading of your paper double-checking your grammar, spelling, organization, and the clarity of your ideas.

LESSON TWENTY

Objectives
1. To broaden students' knowledge regarding ancient Egypt
2. To allow students to practice public speaking skills
3. To allow students to interact to compose a final group project
4. To allow students to determine how their project fits into a larger unit of study

Activity
Choose one of the groups to go first with their group presentations, or allow groups to volunteer. Each group should begin by offering an overview of the topic and presenting the final project. Following each presentation, the class should have an opportunity to ask questions to the group.

Follow-up
If you choose, and if time allows, you may follow up the presentations with a discussion of the projects as a whole: *Playing our Egypt Game: What was it like?*
Compare/contrast the class experience with the experience portrayed in the novel. Brainstorm and discuss responses as time and interest permit. Where in your community could "Egypt" exist? Would an "Egypt Game" work in our community in the 21st century? How was our game different from the players' game in the novel (for example, the students in your class did not *choose* Egypt as a topic).

LESSON TWENTY-ONE

Objective
To review the main ideas and events in *The Egypt Game*

Activity
Choose one of the review games/activities suggested in this unit and spend your class time as directed there.

REVIEW GAMES/ACTIVITIES *The Egypt Game*

1. Ask the class to make up a unit test for *The Egypt Game*. The test should have 4 sections: matching, true/false, short answer, and essay. Students may use 1/2 period to make the test and then swap papers and use the other 1/2 class period to take a test a classmate has devised. (open book). You may want to use the unit test included in this packet or take questions from the students' unit tests to formulate your own test.

2. Take 1/2 period for students to make up true and false questions (including the answers). Collect the papers and divide the class into two teams. Draw a big tic-tac-toe board on the chalk board. Make one team X and one team O. Ask questions to each side, giving each student one turn. If the question is answered correctly, that students' team's letter (X or O) is placed in the box. If the answer is incorrect, no letter is placed in the box. The object is to get three in a row like tic-tac-toe. You may want to keep track of the number of games won for each team.

3. Take 1/2 period for students to make up questions (true/false and short answer). Collect the questions. Divide the class into two teams. You'll alternate asking questions to individual members of teams A & B (like in a spelling bee). The question keeps going from A to B until it is correctly answered, then a new question is asked. A correct answer does not allow the team to get another question. Correct answers are +2 points; incorrect answers are -1 point.

4. Have students pair up and quiz each other from their study guides and class notes.

5. Give students an *The Egypt Game* crossword puzzle to complete.

6. Divide your class into two teams. Use *The Egypt Game* crossword words with their letters jumbled as a word list. Student 1 from Team A faces off against Student 1 from Team B. You write the first jumbled word on the board. The first student (1A or 1B) to unscramble the word wins the chance for his/her team to score points. If 1A wins the jumble, go to student 2A and give him/her a clue. He/she must give you the correct word which matches that clue. If he/she does, Team A scores a point, and you give student 3A a clue for which you expect another correct response. Continue giving Team A clues until some team member makes an incorrect response. An incorrect response sends the game back to the jumbled-word face off, this time with students 2A and 2B. Instead of repeating giving clues to the first few students of each team, continue with the student after the one who gave the last incorrect response on the team. For example, if Team B wins the jumbled-word face-off, and student 5B gave the last incorrect answer for Team B, you would start this round of clue questions with student 6B, and so on. The team with the most points wins!

Review Games Page 2

8. Play What's My Line?. This is similar to the old television show. Students assume the roles of different characters from the novel. One student gives clues to the class, or to a panel of contestants. The contestants try to guess the identity of the guest. Students may enjoy assisting you in creating rules and procedures for the game.

9. Play Jeopardy. Divide the class into two groups. Assign each group a category from the novel and have them devise answers for that category. Play the game according to the television show procedures.

10. Play Drawing in the Details. This is similar to Pictionary. Divide students into teams. A student from one team draws a scene from the novel. (You may want to specify the chapter.) Drawings should be kept simple, to keep the pace lively. Students on the opposing team locate the scene in their books and read it aloud. If they are incorrect, the illustrator's team has a chance to guess. Involve students in setting up a scoring system and any other necessary rules.

UNIT TESTS

SHORT ANSWER UNIT TEST 1 - *The Egypt Game*

I. Matching/Identify

____ 1. February   A. Elizabeth's pet

____ 2. Imagery   B. Figurative language characterized by vivid description

____ 3. Reading   C. April's nickname

____ 4. Library   D. Word choice

____ 5. Allusion   E. Caroline's place of work

____ 6. Oracle   F. In literature, an indirect reference to something found outside of the work

____ 7. Thoth   G. April's and Melanie's next topic of study?

____ 8. Archaeologist   H. The study of man and his culture

____ 9. Anthropology   I. Melanie's favorite past-time

____ 10. Diction   J. Serves as the oracle in the players' Egypt

____ 11. Demonstrations   K. The players raise money to purchase _____

____ 12. Bastet   L. Toby uses Petey to demonstrate this process

____ 13. Mummification   M. April's Egyptian name

____ 14. Petey   N. April's communication with Dorothea is through ____

____ 15. Gypsies   O. Answers questions for the players that no one would know

____ 16. Colored pens   P. April claims she wants to be one of these when she grows up

____ 17. Letters   Q. Non-violent method of protest

____ 18. Professor   R. Frequently watches the players throughout *The Egypt Game*

____ 19. Mr. Schmitt   S. Apartment building where several of the characters live

____ 20. Casa Rosada   T. Owns the local variety store

The Egypt Game Short Answer Unit Test 1 Page 2

II. Short Answer

1. Who owns the curio store?

2. Who is Dorothea?

3. What does April purchase from the drugstore?

4. What does April tell the owner of the curio shop she wants to be when she grows up?

5. Why doesn't April think Melanie will like her?

6. Where do the girls get the rules for the Egypt game?

7. What do Isis and Nefertiti represent?

8. Who organizes the efforts to invite the Professor to leave the community?

9. Who do the girls run into while trick-or-treating?

The Egypt Game Short Answer Unit Test 1 Page 3

10. What does Marshall mumble under his breath after April tells him not to yell (while they are in Egypt)?

11. What kind of list does Toby ask the girls to make?

12. Why does Toby think they should finish the alphabet of hieroglyphics?

13. What knowledge does "one very small Egyptian" hold that he chooses not to share with the others?

14. What does Marshall ask the oracle?

15. What does Toby confess to April and Melanie during their conversation at school?

16. What happens to April after she climbs through the board in the fence on the night she returns to Egypt with Marshall?

The Egypt Game Short Answer Unit Test 1 Page 4

17. Who finally calls for help after the incident described in question #16?

18. What does April call Caroline for the first time after being questioned by the police?

19. How does the experience with April change Marshall's behavior towards the end of the novel?

20. How does April respond to Dorothea's letter of invitation just before Christmas?

21. What information does the Professor give about the oracle?

22. What does the Professor give to each member of the Egypt gang?

23. What are the Professor's plans for the future?

24. What is the Professor's real name?

25. Why does April feel sad towards the end of the book?

The Egypt Game Short Answer Unit Test 1 Page 5

III. Essay

"Melanie looked at April curiously. She'd noticed before that April, in spite of her sophisticated ways, really didn't know much at all about certain kinds of things. The kinds of things parents tell their children when they're alone together and other kids tell you if they know you really well. All April's information seemed to be the kind of things grown-ups let you overhear, and of course, nearly everything she could find in the children's part of libraries."

What does this passage tell the reader about April and Melanie? How have their childhoods differed?

The Egypt Game Short Answer Unit Test 1 Page 6

IV. Vocabulary

    Write down the vocabulary words. Go back later and write down the correct definition for each word.

1.

2.

3.

4.

5.

6.

7.

8.

9.

10.

SHORT ANSWER UNIT TEST 1 ANSWER KEY - *The Egypt Game*

I. Matching/Identify

1. C	11. Q
2. B	12. M
3. I	13. L
4. E	14. A
5. F	15. G
6. O	16. K
7. J	17. N
8. P	18. R
9. H	19. T
10. D	20. S

II. Short Answer

1. Who owns the curio store?
    The Professor

2. Who is Dorothea?
    April's mother

3. What does April purchase from the drug store?
    False eyelashes, as well as a few other items

4. What does April tell the owner of the curio shop she wants to be when she grows up?
    Archaeologist

5. Why doesn't April think Melanie will like her?
    Most kids don't

6. Where do the girls get the rules for the Egypt game?
    They make them up as they go along

7. What do Isis and Nefertiti represent?
    Love, beauty, and perfection

8. Who organizes the efforts to invite the Professor to leave the community?
    Mr. Schmitt

9. Who do the girls run into while trick-or-treating?
    Toby Alvillar and Ken Kamata

10. What does Marshall mumble under his breath after April tells him not to yell while they are in Egypt?
    "Somebody already heard us."

11. What kind of list does Toby ask the girls to make?
    The best books about Egypt

12. Why does Toby think they should finish the alphabet of hieroglyphics?
    In order to communicate in secret code while also being more authentic

13. What knowledge does "one very small Egyptian" hold that he chooses not to share with the others?
    He knows that the Land of Egypt is being watched

14. What does Marshall ask the oracle?
    Where is Security?

15. What does Toby confess to April and Melanie during their conversation at school?
    He has been answering the questions posed to the oracle, but he doesn't have the answer to Marshall's, which concerns him

16. What happens to April after she climbs through the board in the fence on the night she returns to Egypt with Marshall?
    She is attacked/grabbed

17. Who finally calls for help when April is being attacked?
    A strange voice (which belongs to the Professor/Dr. Huddleston)

18. What does April call Caroline for the first time after being questioned by police?
    Grandma

19. How does the experience with April change Marshall's behavior?
    He no longer takes Security with him *everywhere* he goes

20. How does April respond to Dorothea's letter of invitation just before Christmas?
    She declines her invitation to visit

21. What information does the Professor give about the oracle?
    He answered the question Marshall posed to the oracle because he wanted Marshall to be able to find his beloved Security.

22. What does the Professor give to each member of the Egypt gang?
    A key

23. What are the Professor's plans for the future?
    He will begin importing, traveling, and selling goods again.

24. What is the Professor's real name?
    Dr. Huddleston

25. Why does April feel sad towards the end of the book?
    She is afraid that Egypt will not be the same when they return...that the disappointment will ruin the "remembering."

SHORT ANSWER UNIT TEST 2 - *The Egypt Game*

I. Matching/Identify

____ 1. February   A. Owns the local variety store

____ 2. Imagery   B. Apartment building where several of the characters live

____ 3. Reading   C. Frequently watches the players throughout the Egypt Game

____ 4. Library   D. Non-violent method of protest

____ 5. Allusion   E. April claims she wants to be one of these when she grows up

____ 6. Oracle   F. Answers questions for the players that no one would know

____ 7. Thoth   G. April's communication with Dorothea is through _____

____ 8. Archaeologist   H. April's Egyptian name

____ 9. Anthropology   I. Toby uses Petey to demonstrate this process

____ 10. Diction   J. The players raise money to purchase _____

____ 11. Demonstrations   K. Serves as the oracle in the players' Egypt

____ 12. Bastet   L. Melanie's favorite past-time

____ 13. Mummification   M. The study of man and his culture

____ 14. Petey   N. April's and Melanie's next topic of study?

____ 15. Gypsies   O. In literature, an indirect reference to something found outside of the work

____ 16. Colored pens   P. Caroline's place of work

____ 17. Letters   Q. Word choice

____ 18. Professor   R. April's nickname

____ 19. Mr. Schmitt   S. Figurative language characterized by vivid description

____ 20. Casa Rosada   T. Elizabeth's pet

The Egypt Game Short Answer Unit Test 2 Page 2

II. Short Answer

1. What does Marshall always carry with him?

2. Who is Caroline?

3. What happened to April's father?

4. Why is April impressed by the man at A-Z?

5. What is Melanie's reaction to April when she meets her for the first time?

6. What activity makes April decide to take off her eyelashes (at least temporarily)?

7. What reason does April first give Melanie about her feelings about Caroline?

8. Who is Set?

9. Why is Melanie having trouble concentrating the day before school starts?

The Egypt Game Short Answer Unit Test 2 Page 3

10. Who does Elizabeth look like to April and Melanie?

11. Under what circumstances are the kids in the neighborhood allowed to trick-or-treat?

12. What are the Egyptians looking for as they are trick-or-treating?

13. What does the Egypt gang claim is the secret omen?

14. Why does Elizabeth ask Toby and Ken to join their game?

15. Who is Petey?

16. What initially gets the players' interested in the topic of the oracle?

17. What is the first question that Ken asks the oracle?

18. Why does Toby call April at home (even though it goes against his principles)?

The Egypt Game Short Answer Unit Test 2 Page 4

19. What does April wonder about Marshall's behavior as she is being attacked?

20. Where do April and Marshall go immediately after April is attacked?

21. How does Marshall describe the man who grabs April?

22. What happens to the land of Egypt after April is attacked?

23. Why does the Christmas Eve visitor say he would like to meet with the Egypt gang?

24. What does the Professor give to each member of the Egypt gang?

25. What question does April pose to Melanie at the end of the novel?

The Egypt Game Short Answer Unit Test 2 Page 5

III. Composition

"It had been a place to get away to–a private lair–a secret seclusion meant to be shared with best friends only–a life unknown to grown-ups and lived by kids alone."

How does the above quote apply to Egypt? Is it accurate? What does it say about the relationships shared by the members of the Egypt gang?

The Egypt Game Short Answer Unit Test 2 Page 6

IV. Vocabulary

    Write down the vocabulary words. Go back later and write down the correct definitions for the words.

1.

2.

3.

4.

5.

6.

7.

8.

9.

10.

SHORT ANSWER UNIT TEST 2: ANSWER KEY - *The Egypt Game*

I. Matching/Identify

1. R	11. D
2. S	12. H
3. L	13. I
4. P	14. T
5. O	15. N
6. F	16. J
7. K	17. G
8. E	18. C
9. M	19. A
10. Q	20. B

II. Short Answer

1. What does Marshall always carry with him?
    Security- a huge octopus

2. Who is Caroline?
    April's paternal grandmother

3. What happened to April's father?
    He died before April ever had a chance to know him

4. Why is April impressed by the man at A-Z?
    He is able to maintain a deadpan expression

5. What is Melanie's reaction to April when she meets her for the first time?
    She is speechless

6. What activity makes April decide to take off her eyelashes (at least temporarily)?
    They interfere with her ability to read

7. What reason does April first give Melanie about her feelings about Caroline?
    She says Caroline doesn't like Dorothea; she is also angry that Caroline seems doubtful that Dorothea will send for her to come back "home" soon

8. Who is Set?
    The god of evil and black magic

9. Why is Melanie having trouble concentrating the day before school starts?
    She is worried about her plan to steal April's eyelashes

10. Who does Elizabeth look like to April and Melanie?
    Nefertiti

11. Under what circumstances are the kids in the neighborhood allowed to trick-or-treat?
    They are chaperoned by the kids' fathers

12. What are the Egyptians looking for as they are trick-or-treating?
    A secret omen

13. What does the Egypt gang claim is the secret omen?
    A shooting star

14. Why does Elizabeth ask Toby and Ken to join their game?
    To keep them from tattling on their secret Egypt

15. Who is Petey?
    Elizabeth's pet parakeet

16. What initially gets the players' interested in the topic of the oracle?
    A discussion in Mrs. Granger's sixth grade class

17. What is the first question that Ken asks the oracle?
    "Will I be a big league star someday?"

18. Why does Toby call April at home (even though it goes against his principles)?
    To set up a meeting at school the next day

19. What does April wonder about Marshall's behavior as she is being attacked?
    She wonders why he isn't calling for help

20. Where do April and Marshall go immediately after April is attacked?
    The police station

21. How does Marshall describe the man who grabs April?
    "Old," "big man," with "orange hair and spotted skin"

22. What happens to the land of Egypt after April is attacked?
    It is boarded up

23. Why does the Christmas Eve visitor say he would like to meet with the Egypt gang?
    To tell them a story

24. What does the Professor give to each member of the Egypt gang?
    A key to Egypt

25. What question does April pose to Melanie at the end of the novel?
    "Melanie, what do you know about Gypsies?"

ADVANCED SHORT ANSWER UNIT TEST - *The Egypt Game*

I. Matching/Identify

____ 1. February   A. Owns the local variety store

____ 2. Imagery   B. Apartment building where several of the characters live

____ 3. Reading   C. Frequently watches the players throughout the Egypt Game

____ 4. Library   D. Non-violent method of protest

____ 5. Allusion   E. April claims she wants to be one of these when she grows up

____ 6. Oracle   F. Answers questions for the players that no one would know

____ 7. Thoth   G. April's communication with Dorothea is through _____

____ 8. Archaeologist   H. April's Egyptian name

____ 9. Anthropology   I. Toby uses Petey to demonstrate this process

____ 10. Diction   J. The players raise money to purchase _____

____ 11. Demonstrations   K. Serves as the oracle in the players' Egypt

____ 12. Bastet   L. Melanie's favorite past-time

____ 13. Mummification   M. The study of man and his culture

____ 14. Petey   N. April's and Melanie's next topic of study?

____ 15. Gypsies   O. In literature, an indirect reference to something found outside of the work

____ 16. Colored pens   P. Caroline's place of work

____ 17. Letters   Q. Word choice

____ 18. Professor   R. April's nickname

____ 19. Mr. Schmitt   S. Figurative language characterized by vivid description

____ 20. Casa Rosada   T. Elizabeth's pet

The Egypt Game Advanced Short Answer Unit Test Page 2

II. Vocabulary

    Write down the vocabulary words. Go back later and write down the correct definition for each word.

1.

2.

3.

4.

5.

6.

7.

8.

9.

10.

11.

12.

The Egypt Game Advanced Short Answer Unit Test Page 3

III. Short Answer/Quotations

Choose 10 of the following quotes and explain the importance of each to the novel. Consider our class discussions, as well as your own thoughts. Use a few sentences for each quote.

1. "And one of the things they had in common, at that time, was a vague and mysterious fear of the old man called the Professor."

2. He didn't talk very much, but when he did he always said exactly what he wanted to without any trouble."

3. "There was only one thing that April didn't seem to know much about–that was getting along with people."

4. "But even without the eyelashes Melanie had a hard time trying to translate April into something that Wilson School could understand and appreciate."

The Egypt Game Advanced Short Answer Unit Test Page 4

5. "So when they started calling April, February, Melanie knew that everything would be all right."

6. "And there was something about the carved perfection of her face that made her smile seem like magic–an enchanted ivory princess warming suddenly to life."

7. "She'd noticed before that April, in spite of her sophisticated ways, really didn't know much at all about certain kinds of things. The kinds of things parents tell their children when they're alone together and other kids tell you if they know you really well. All April's information seemed to be the kind of things grown-ups let you overhear, and of course, nearly everything she could find in the children's part of libraries."

8. "Both the bigger girls looked surprised. Elizabeth wasn't the kind of person you expect to come up with ideas in an emergency."

9. "But Toby shook his head. "I don't feel like playing basketball," he said. "Besides, I sort of go for this Egypt stuff. Let's hang around awhile. Okay?"

The Egypt Game Advanced Short Answer Unit Test Page 5

10. "After all," Toby said, "Thoth was the Egyptian god of wisdom, and this crazy priestess bit was something the Greeks thought up."

11. "Lie to you!" Toby said. "I did not. I didn't lie to you once. I just gave the wrong impression. There's a difference."

12. "Well," April and Melanie said to each other–only just with a look, not out loud, "wasn't that like a boy. They got things into a mess and then expected a girl to get them out of it."

13. "Marshall for some reason had turned around and was aiming the light in the opposite direction, on the wall of the Professor's store, but at her whisper he turned back."

The Egypt Game Advanced Short Answer Unit Test Page 6

14. "He said Security didn't want his picture taken. After that he started leaving Security home sometimes when he went places, and before too long, he didn't need to have Security with him at all anymore, excepting to hold on to at night when he was sleepy."

15. "It had been a place to get away to–a private lair–a secret seclusion meant to be shared with best friends only–a life unknown to grown-ups and lived by kids alone."

The Egypt Game Advanced Short Answer Unit Test Page 7
IV. Composition

Choose 2 of the following questions to discuss. Consider our class discussions, as well as your own conclusions about the novel. Be sure to cite specific examples from the novel to support your essay. You may use the blank pages at the end of this exam to complete your answers.

1. How is the Egypt Game a "game" in the traditional sense? How is it different?

2. Do you believe the Egypt gang would have been friends if they had not shared a common interest and a common experience? Explain. Be sure to discuss each of the players in your explanation.

3. What does Egppt become for each of the characters? (choose 4 characters for your discussion).

4. Why are April's eyelashes important in the novel? What do they tell us about April? What do they symbolize?

5. What roles do the parents and guardians play in this novel? Compare and contrast the different parents in the novel and note how they influence their children.

MULTIPLE CHOICE UNIT TEST 1 - *The Egypt Game*

I. Matching

____ 1. February A. Elizabeth's pet

____ 2. Imagery B. Figurative language characterized by vivid description

____ 3. Reading C. April's nickname

____ 4. Library D. Word choice

____ 5. Allusion E. Caroline's place of work

____ 6. Oracle F. In literature, an indirect reference to something found outside of the work

____ 7. Thoth G. April's and Melanie's next topic of study?

____ 8. Archaeologist H. The study of man and his culture

____ 9. Anthropology I. Melanie's favorite past-time

____ 10. Diction J. Serves as the oracle in the players' Egypt

____ 11. Demonstrations K. The players raise money to purchase _____

____ 12. Bastet L. Toby uses Petey to demonstrate this process

____ 13. Mummification M. April's Egyptian name

____ 14. Petey N. April's communication with Dorothea is through ____

____ 15. Gypsies O. Answers questions for the players that no one would know

____ 16. Colored pens P. April claims she wants to be one of these when she grows up

____ 17. Letters Q. Non-violent method of protest

____ 18. Professor R. Frequently watches the players throughout the Egypt Game

____ 19. Mr. Schmitt S. Apartment building where several of the characters live

____ 20. Casa Rosada T. Owns the local variety store

The Egypt Game Multiple Choice Unit Test 1 Page 2

II. Multiple Choice

1. Who owns the curio store?
    A. the state of California
    B. the Professor
    C. Nefertiti
    D. the university

2. Who is Dorothea?
    A. April's mother
    B. April's sister
    C. April's cat
    D. April's aunt

3. What does April purchase from the drugstore?
    A. a heating pad
    B. lipstick
    C. false eyelashes
    D. a magazine

4. What does April tell the owner of the curio shop she wants to be when she grows up?
    A. an actress
    B. Miss America
    C. a doctor
    D. an archaeologist

5. Why doesn't April think Melanie will like her?
    A. Kids usually don't like April.
    B. They have always fought with one another.
    C. They are rivals on opposite soccer teams.
    D. They have nothing in common.

6. Where do the girls get the rules for the Egypt game?
    A. They found them on scrolls inside the statue of Nefertiti.
    B. They invent them as they play.
    C. The found the rules in a book from the library.
    D. Mr. Ross outlines the rules.

7. What do Isis and Nefertiti represent?
    A. faith and hope
    B. wisdom and intellect
    C. love, beauty, and perfection
    D. strength and devotion

The Egypt Game Multiple Choice Unit Test 1 Page 3

8. Who organizes the efforts to invite the Professor to leave the community?
    A. Mr. Schmitt
    B. Caroline
    C. Dorothea
    D. The Rosses

9. Who do the girls run into while trick-or-treating?
    A. the Professor
    B. Dorothea
    C. Toby Alvillar and Ken Kamata
    D. Caroline

10. What does Marshall mumble under his breath after April tells him not to yell in Egypt?
    A. "I wasn't yelling."
    B. "You're not my boss."
    C. "Somebody already heard us."
    D. "Well, you were yelling, too."

11. What kind of list does Toby ask the girls to make?
    A. a list of all the kids in the class with their phone numbers
    B. a list of the best books about Egypt
    C. a list of pizza places in the neighborhood
    D. a list of the funniest movies they have ever seen

12. Why does Toby think they should finish the alphabet of hieroglyphics?
    A. so they can make t-shirts with it
    B. so they can make copies for their class at school
    C. as extra-credit for social studies
    D. so they can use it as a secret code outside of Egypt

13. What knowledge does "one very small Egyptian" hold that he chooses not to share with the others?
    A. He knows that the Land of Egypt is being watched.
    B. He knows the answer to the Riddle of the Sphynx.
    C. He knows who killed Cock Robin.
    D. He learns that the chicken came before the egg.

14. What does Marshall ask the oracle?
    A. "Where is Security?"
    B. "Where are my tennis shoes?"
    C. "What will I get for Christmas?"
    D. "Where will I go to elementary school?"

The Egypt Game Multiple Choice Unit Test 1 Page 4

15. What does Toby confess to April and Melanie during their conversation at school?
    A. that he told his friends about Egypt
    B. that he has never liked basketball
    C. that he has been acting as the oracle, but doesn't know how to help Marshall
    D. that he lost the books about Egypt that they lent to him

16. What happens to April after she climbs through the board in the fence on the night she returns to Egypt with Marshall?
    A. she cuts her leg on the fence
    B. she falls into a rain puddle
    C. someone grabs her
    D. she tears her sweater

17. Who finally calls for help on the night April and Marshall return to Egypt alone?
    A. Marshall
    B. April
    C. Melanie
    D. a strange voice

18. After her visit to the police station, what does April call Caroline for the first time?
    A. Ms. Caroline
    B. Mom
    C. Grandma
    D. her friend

19. How does the scary experience with April change Marshall's behavior at the end of the novel?
    A. He is afraid to leave the apartment alone.
    B. He no longer takes Security with him everywhere he goes.
    C. He cries all the time.
    D. Nothing changes.

20. How does April respond to Dorothea's letter she receives just before Christmas?
    A. She declines the invitation to visit Dorothea
    B. She tells Dorothea she is ready to move back in with Dorothea and Nick
    C. She does not respond at all
    D. She asks Dorothea not to write to her anymore

The Egypt Game Multiple Choice Unit Test 1 Page 5

21. What information does the Professor give the Egypt gang about the oracle when he meets with them on Christmas Eve?
    A. He tore down the oracle after April's attack.
    B. He believes the oracle is magical.
    C. He answered Marshall's question to help him find Security.
    D. He does not mention the oracle.

22. What does the Professor give to each member of the Egypt gang?
    A. a fruitcake
    B. a key
    C. a book
    D. an artifact from his store

23. What are the Professor's plans for the future?
    A. He will begin importing, traveling, and selling goods again.
    B. He and Caroline are getting married.
    C. He is moving his home and shop to Delaware.
    D. He will begin teaching at the university in the fall.

24. What is the Professor's real name?
    A. Bob Tanner
    B. Captain Paulsen
    C. Dr. Huddleston
    D. Michael Townsend

25. Why does April feel sad at the end of the novel?
    A. She will miss her friends when she moves back with Dorothea.
    B. She will miss the Professor.
    C. She fears that returning to Egypt will be a disappointment.
    D. She has lost her eyelashes.

The Egypt Game Multiple Choice Unit Test 1 Page 6

III. Composition

1. How does April's relationship with Caroline change throughout the novel? What events bring about these changes? Cite specific examples.

2. Why are the eyelashes important at the beginning of the novel? What do they tell us about April? What do they symbolize?

3. How do the "rules" and "procedures" of the Egypt Game change as each new player is added? Do you think the game improves as the group expands?

4. What does Egypt become to the Professor and each of the players?

The Egypt Game Multiple Choice Unit Test 1 Page 7

IV. Vocabulary - Match the correct definitions to the words.

____ 1. balefully   A. called together

____ 2. pomp   B. revealed

____ 3. integrate   C. to consider one's success with smugness

____ 4. prostration   D. ominously, threateningly

____ 5. evasive   E. a sign that predicts a future event

____ 6. liable   F. the study of man and his society and culture

____ 7. disclosed   G. dismay

____ 8. faltered   H. big, showy display

____ 9. principles   I. A medium for divine prophecy

____ 10. gloat   J. to bring together into a whole

____ 11. summoned   K. position of being stretched out on the ground

____ 12. anthropology   L. opportunity

____ 13. oracle   M. wavered, hesitated

____ 14. prospect   N. set of personal beliefs that guides one's behavior

____ 15. seldom   O. way to spend time

____ 16. consternation   P. infrequent

____ 17. omen   Q. an opinion shared by a group

____ 18. occupation   R. likely, apt

____ 19. consensus   S. the study of physical remains/excavation sites to study humans

____ 20. archaeology   T. deliberately seeking to avoid through cleverness

ANSWER KEY - *The Egypt Game*
Multiple Choice Unit Test 1

I. Matching	II. Multiple Choice	IV. Vocabulary
1. C	1. B	1. D
2. B	2. A	2. H
3. I	3. C	3. J
4. E	4. D	4. K
5. F	5. A	5. T
6. O	6. B	6. R
7. J	7. C	7. B
8. P	8. A	8. M
9. H	9. C	9. N
10. D	10. C	10. C
11. Q	11. B	11. A
12. M	12. D	12. F
13. L	13. A	13. I
14. A	14. A	14. L
15. G	15. C	15. P
16. K	16. C	16. G
17. N	17. D	17. E
18. R	18. C	18. O
19. T	19. B	19. Q
20. S	20. A	20. S
	21. C	
	22. B	
	23. A	
	24. C	
	25. C	

MULTIPLE CHOICE UNIT TEST 2 - *The Egypt Game*

I. Matching

____ 1. February   A. Owns the local variety store

____ 2. Imagery   B. Apartment building where several of the characters live

____ 3. Reading   C. Frequently watches the players throughout the Egypt Game

____ 4. Library   D. Non-violent method of protest

____ 5. Allusion   E. April claims she wants to be one of these when she grows up

____ 6. Oracle   F. Answers questions for the players that no one would know

____ 7. Thoth   G. April's communication with Dorothea is through _____

____ 8. Archaeologist   H. April's Egyptian name

____ 9. Anthropology   I. Toby uses Petey to demonstrate this process

____ 10. Diction   J. The players raise money to purchase _____

____ 11. Demonstrations   K. Serves as the oracle in the players' Egypt

____ 12. Bastet   L. Melanie's favorite past-time

____ 13. Mummification   M. The study of man and his culture

____ 14. Petey   N. April's and Melanie's next topic of study?

____ 15. Gypsies   O. In literature, an indirect reference to something found outside of the work

____ 16. Colored pens   P. Caroline's place of work

____ 17. Letters   Q. Word choice

____ 18. Professor   R. April's nickname

____ 19. Mr. Schmitt   S. Figurative language characterized by vivid description

____ 20. Casa Rosada   T. Elizabeth's pet

The Egypt Game Multiple Choice Unit Test 2 Page 2

II. Multiple Choice

1. What does Marshall always carry with him?
    A. a flashlight
    B. his lunch
    C. a blanket
    D. a stuffed octopus

2. Who is Caroline?
    A. April's best friend
    B. April's grandmother
    C. April's cat
    D. April's twin sister

3. What happened to April's father?
    A. He was arrested.
    B. He got lost on the interstate.
    C. He broke his thumb.
    D. He died in an accident before April knew him.

4. Why is April impressed by the man at A-Z?
    A. He has a deadpan expression.
    B. He has so many beautiful things.
    C. He knows her name.
    D. He is a famous movie star.

5. What is Melanie's initial reaction to April?
    A. She is frightened and starts to tremble.
    B. She laughs at the scene before her.
    C. She is speechless.
    D. She becomes angry.

6. What makes April finally take off her eyelashes (at least temporarily)?
    A. Her teacher doesn't allow her to wear them.
    B. They make reading difficult.
    C. She loses one of them.
    D. She decides to wear sunglasses instead.

7. What reason does April give Melanie for her feelings about Caroline?
    A. She appreciates the fact that Caroline allows her to stay with her.
    B. She had never met Caroline before coming to the Casa Rosada.
    C. Caroline is a mean and stingy woman.
    D. Caroline does not like Dorothea and doesn't believe Dorothea will send for her.

The Egypt Game Multiple Choice Unit Test 2 Page 3

8. Who is Set?
    A. the god of wisdom and intellect
    B. the god of beauty and love
    C. the god of humor and laughter
    D. the god of evil and black magic

9. Why is April having trouble concentrating the day before school is to begin?
    A. She has the flu.
    B. She is getting ready to move to another state.
    C. She is remembering that Dorothea promised to bring her home soon.
    D. She is so excited about making new friends.

10. Who does Elizabeth look like to April and Melanie?
    A. Miss America
    B. Nefertiti
    C. another friend from the Casa Rosada
    D. April's mother

11. Under what circumstances are the kids in the neighborhood allowed to trick-or-treat?
    A. They are chaperoned by some of the fathers.
    B. They may only trick-or-treat inside the apartment complex.
    C. The murderer has been arrested.
    D. The kids are accompanied by a policeman.

12. What are the players watching for as they trick-or-treat?
    A. someone dressed as Frankenstein
    B. a funny jack-o-lantern
    C. a secret omen that will cue them to return to Egypt
    D. Marshall's Security

13. What does the Egypt gang claim is the secret omen?
    A. a funny jack-o-lantern
    B. a shooting star
    C. a bag full of Tootsie Rolls
    D. a full moon

14. Why does Elizabeth invite Toby and Ken to join their game?
    A. She has to, to keep them from telling an adult about Egypt.
    B. They have been wanting some more male actors.
    C. She has a crush on Toby.
    D. She asks before she even thinks about it.

The Egypt Game Multiple Choice Unit Test 2 Page 4

15. Who is Petey?
    A. Toby's twin brother
    B. Melanie's cat
    C. Elizabeth's pet parakeet that dies
    D. the Professor

16. What gets the gang interested in the topic of the oracle?
    A. a discussion about oracles in Mrs. Granger's sixth grade class
    B. a comment made by Mr. Ross
    C. an article in the newspaper
    D. a scene from a movie

17. What is the first question Ken asks the oracle?
    A. "Where did I leave my wallet?"
    B. "Will I be a big league star someday?"
    C. "Will I pass my math test tomorrow?"
    D. "What will I get for my birthday?"

18. Why does Toby call April at home?
    A. He wants to ask her to the movies.
    B. He has a question about his math homework.
    C. To set up a meeting at school the next day.
    D. He does it as a practical joke.

19. What does April wonder about Marshall's behavior as she is being attacked?
    A. She wonders if he is safe.
    B. She wonders why he isn't calling for help.
    C. She wonders if he went back to the apartment ahead of her.
    D. She wonders if he is scared.

20. Where do Marshall and April go immediately after April is attacked?
    A. They are taken to the police station.
    B. Caroline takes them to McDonald's.
    C. They go to the drug store.
    D. They go to the airport.

21. How does Marshall describe the man who grabs April?
    A. Marshall says he is a "big man," "old," with "orange hair and spotted skin."
    B. Marshall says that he looks like the Professor.
    C. Marshall says he is "a young man wearing purple pants."
    D. He did not see the man.

The Egypt Game Multiple Choice Unit Test 2 Page 5

22. What happens to the land of Egypt after April is attacked?
    A. A storm destroys it all.
    B. The parents clear everything out and throw it all away.
    C. Nothing-the gang resumes the Egypt Game immediately.
    D. It is boarded up.

23. What reason does the Christmas Eve visitor give for wanting to meet with the group?
    A. He has come to tell them a story.
    B. He wants to meet all of them in person.
    C. He has nowhere else to spend the holiday.
    D. He wants to return Security.

24. What does the Professor give to each member of the Egypt gang?
    A. a fruitcake
    B. a key
    C. a book
    D. an artifact from his store

25. What question does April pose to Melanie at the end of the novel?
    A. "Melanie, what do you know about Gypsies?"
    B. "Melanie, will you come visit me at Dorothea's?"
    C. "Melanie, what would you like for dinner?"
    D. "Melanie, would you like to go to the playground?"

The Egypt Game Multiple Choice Unit Test 2 Page 6

III. Composition

1. What causes Toby to confess his actions about the oracle to Melanie and April? What does this tell the reader about Toby?

2. How do the "rules" and "procedures" of the Egypt Game change as each new player is added? Do you think the game improves as the group expands?

3. How does April's relationship with Caroline change throughout the novel? What events bring about these changes?

The Egypt Game Multiple Choice Unit Test 2 Page 7

IV. Vocabulary - Match the correct definitions to the words.

    ____ 1. Offset   A. Showy display

    ____ 2. Clamored   B. Ominously; threateningly

    ____ 3. Relish   C. Way to spend time

    ____ 4. Balefully   D. Demanded loudly

    ____ 5. Speculated   E. Secret meeting

    ____ 6. Lair   F. Mutual agreement

    ____ 7. Primitive   G. Able to write or speak easily

    ____ 8. Abandon   H. A state of quiet separation from others

    ____ 9. Pomp   I. Compensate for

    ____ 10. Rendezvous   J. Infrequent

    ____ 11. Accord   K. Bring together into a whole

    ____ 12. Warily   L. Seeking to avoid through cleverness

    ____ 13. Integrate   M. Formed a theory without much evidence

    ____ 14. Drone   N. Relating to man's earliest existence

    ____ 15. Seclusion   O. Absence of inhibitions and restraint

    ____ 16. Anthropology   P. A hiding place

    ____ 17. Occupation   Q. Great enjoyment

    ____ 18. Seldom   R. Study of man and his culture and religion

    ____ 19. Fluent   S. A constant low humming sound

    ____ 20. Evasive   T. Acting with caution

ANSWER SHEET - *The Egypt Game*
Multiple Choice Unit Tests

I. Matching	II. Multiple Choice	IV. Vocabulary
1. ___	1. ___	1. ___
2. ___	2. ___	2. ___
3. ___	3. ___	3. ___
4. ___	4. ___	4. ___
5. ___	5. ___	5. ___
6. ___	6. ___	6. ___
7. ___	7. ___	7. ___
8. ___	8. ___	8. ___
9. ___	9. ___	9. ___
10. ___	10. ___	10. ___
11. ___	11. ___	11. ___
12. ___	12. ___	12. ___
13. ___	13. ___	13. ___
14. ___	14. ___	14. ___
15. ___	15. ___	15. ___
16. ___	16. ___	16. ___
17. ___	17. ___	17. ___
18. ___	18. ___	18. ___
19. ___	19. ___	19. ___
20. ___	20. ___	20. ___
	21. ___	
	22. ___	
	23. ___	
	24. ___	
	25. ___	

ANSWER KEY - *The Egypt Game*
Multiple Choice Unit Test 2

I. Matching	II. Multiple Choice	IV. Vocabulary
1. R	1. D	1. I
2. S	2. B	2. D
3. L	3. D	3. Q
4. P	4. A	4. B
5. O	5. C	5. M
6. F	6. B	6. P
7. K	7. D	7. N
8. E	8. D	8. O
9. M	9. C	9. A
10. Q	10. B	10. E
11. D	11. A	11. F
12. H	12. C	12. T
13. I	13. B	13. K
14. T	14. A	14. S
15. N	15. C	15. H
16. J	16. A	16. R
17. G	17. B	17. C
18. C	18. C	18. J
19. A	19. B	19. G
20. B	20. A	20. L
	21. A	
	22. D	
	23. A	
	24. B	
	25. A	

UNIT RESOURCE MATERIALS

BULLETIN BOARD IDEAS - *The Egypt Game*

1. Save one corner of the board for the best of students' *The Egypt Game* writing assignments.

2. Take one of the word search puzzles from the extra activities packet and with a marker copy it over in a large size on the bulletin board. Write the clue words to find to one side. Invite students prior to and after class to find the words and circle them on the bulletin board.

3. Write several of the most significant quotations from the book onto the board on brightly colored paper.

4. Make a bulletin board listing the vocabulary words for this unit. As you complete sections of the novel and discuss the vocabulary for each section, write the definitions on the bulletin board. (If your board is one students face frequently, it will help them learn the words.)

5. Post the group projects related to the Egyptian study on the bulletin board, when possible.

6. Find samples of the flowers listed in the novel and post them on the bulletin board. You might also offer students the opportunity for extra credit by having them draw or research these flowers.

7. Post the riddle of the Sphinx on the bulletin board (but do not give away its roots until it is solved). Ask students to solve the riddle.

8. Towards the end of the unit study, post a section of the bulletin board that reads "What do you know about _____?" Students may brainstorm ideas for subsequent projects and bring in samples, articles, or information related to the new topic.

9. Have students bring in photographs of themselves with their own version of "Security" (or illustrations of the items if they are no longer around). The students might also bring in a paragraph or quote from a family member that describes their relationship to the respective items.

10. Track an ongoing news item by posting articles from various newspapers as the story progresses. Students may bring in articles, as well. Similarly, students may choose to create headlines based on events from the novel to post on the bulletin board.

11. Have students track the influence of ancient Egypt on the modern world by bringing in references throughout the unit study (i.e. the song "Walk Like an Egyptian," pyramids in architecture, etc.) to post on the bulletin board.

12. Have each students write or illustrate what they would like to be when they grow up (or bring in an item that represents that profession). Post these responses on the bulletin along with definitions for any unfamiliar occupations.

EXTRA ACTIVITIES - *The Egypt Game*

One of the difficulties in teaching a novel is that all students don't read at the same speed. One student who likes to read may take the book home and finish it in a day or two. Sometimes a few students finish the in-class assignments early. The problem, then, is finding suitable extra activities for students.

One thing that seems to help is to keep a little library in the classroom. For this unit on *The Egypt Game*, you might check out from the school library other novels by Zilpha Keatley Snyder (including the sequel *The Gypsy Game*). Any stories or articles about ancient Egypt, peace demonstrations of the 1960s, Egyptian rituals and mythology, modern Egypt, anthropology, archaeology, primitive art, the opera *Aida,* or costume design would also be appropriate, as would many other selection. Magazines such as *National Geographic* would also be of interest.

Other things you may keep on hand are puzzles. We have made some relating directly to *The Egypt Game* for you. Feel free to duplicate them for your students to use.

Some students may like to draw. You might devise a contest or allow some extra-credit grade for students who draw characters or scenes from *The Egypt Game.* Note, too, that if the students do not want to keep their drawings you may pick up some extra bulletin board materials this way. If you have a contest and you supply the prize (a CD or something like that perhaps), you could, possibly, make the drawing itself a non-returnable entry fee. Students might also draw the initial scene of the Egypt Game and illustrate the transformations that occur as the novel progresses, much like a mural. See the other Bulletin Board Ideas for activities that students may contribute when they have some extra class time (or particular interest in this unit)

The pages which follow contain games, puzzles and worksheets. The keys, when appropriate, immediately follow the puzzle or worksheet. There are two main groups of activities: one group for the unit; that is, generally relating to *The Egypt Game* text, and another group of activities related strictly to *The Egypt Game* vocabulary.

Directions for these games, puzzles and worksheets are self-explanatory. The object here is to provide you with extra materials you may use in any way you choose.

MORE ACTIVITIES - *The Egypt Game*

1. Have students work together to make a time line chronology of the events in the story. Take a large piece of construction paper and on one wall (or however you can physically arrange it in your room), make the events of the story along it. Students may want to add drawings or cut-out pictures to represent the events (as well as a written statement).

2. Have students design a book cover (front and back and inside flaps) for *The Egypt Game.*

3. Have students design a bulletin board (ready to be put up; not just sketched) for *The Egypt Game.*

4. Have students group the chapters together to show the larger structure of the novel. Have them explain why they chose the divisions they made.

5. Have students choose one chapter of the book (with sufficient dialogue) to rewrite as a play. In conjunction with this assignment, have students write a composition explaining the difficulties they encountered in changing from one written form to another.

6. Have students choose a descriptive passage from the novel to post in the room. Students may also choose to illustrate that passage. In conjunction with this assignment, have students describe how the diction and imagery used in the text contributed to the illustration process. Is the mood of the written passage similar to the mood of the illustrated piece?

7. Have students create a scrapbook of *The Egypt Game*: they may stage photography, use drawings instead of photographs, or find illustrations from books or magazines (make sure they understand they must cite sources in this instance). Students should also provide journaling (short written explanations) to chronicle the experiences they portray. Alternately, students might choose to create a scrapbook for one of the families in the novel, the career of one character, or a figure from ancient Egypt (such as Dorothea or Anne Huddleston). This might also be an interesting way for the students to chronicle the experience they had with their Egypt Group.

8. Have students deliver the speeches that they composed for Writing Assignment 3. If students chose opposite sides of a similar issue, they might debate that topic in class.

9. Ask students to bring in their own "Security" items from their childhood, or pictures of themselves with it (you may want to bring in your own, as well–or share your memory of it). Have them talk to family members about their relationship to that item. Discuss the point at which they were willing to part with the item.

10. Have students take on the personae of the characters from the novel and debate a particular aspect of the Egypt game or argue an issue presented in the novel, such as who should be the oracle, or whether or not the Professor should be "invited" to leave the community.

11. Have students write one or more of the following:
    - A letter from themselves to one of the characters in the novel
    - A letter from one character in the novel to another
    - A letter from themselves to a figure from ancient Egypt
    - A letter from one of the characters to a figure from ancient Egypt
    - A letter of their own choosing related to the novel in some way

12. Invite a police detective, newspaper writer, archaeologist, or anthropologist to class to discuss his/her profession. Students should prepare a list of questions for the guest. You may want to study the passages that relate the guest's area of expertise prior to the his or her arrival. Follow-up with a note of appreciation from the students to the guest.

13. Host a career day by inviting members of various professions to your school (may tie in with #12 above). Your class might even host the event for the school as a mini-unit. Consult with students about which professions they would like to see represented, and have students research the final choices, as well as researching their own career goals.

14. Conduct a mock trial of the Mr. Schmitt's relative who is arrested for the murders. This may form the basis for a mini-unit on debate, law, or the justice system.

The Egypt Game Word List

No.	Word	Clue/Definition
1.	AIDA	Melanie's Egyptian name
2.	ALLUSION	An indirect reference to something
3.	APRIL	She eventually gives up her false eyelashes.
4.	ARCHAEOLOGIST	April claimed to want to be come an ___
5.	BASTET	April's Egyptian name
6.	BOOK	Melanie keeps her paper dolls in a geography ___.
7.	CAROLINE	Dorothea's mother-in-law
8.	CEREMONY	The ___ for the Dead
9.	CURIO	Kind of store the Professor owns
10.	DEMONSTRATION	Non-violent method of protest
11.	DIGNITY	Being a baby offended Marshall's
12.	DOROTHEA	Writes letters to April
13.	EGYPT	Place of fascination for April and Melanie
14.	EYELASHES	Melanie stole April's
15.	FEATHER	It was the token Set and Isis sent as a summons.
16.	FEBRUARY	April's nickname
17.	GIRL	A little ___ is murdered, bringing a halt to the Egypt Game.
18.	GRANT	Policeman who investigates April's attack
19.	GYPSIES	Melanie, what do you know about ___?
20.	HEAD	A shrunken one is brought for Set's altar.
21.	HIEROGLYPHICS	Egyptian writing system
22.	HUDDLESTON	The Professor's real last name
23.	IMAGINING	Melanie's games with paper people
24.	ISIS	The Summons from Set and ___
25.	KEN	His Egyptian name is Horemheb.
26.	KEYS	The Professor gives these to the players
27.	LIBRARY	Caroline's place of work
28.	MARSHAMOSIS	Name of the gang's first pharaoh
29.	MELANIE	Identifies with the title character from Aida
30.	MUMMIFICATION	Preservation of dead bodies
31.	NEFERTITI	Elizabeth reminded the girls of her
32.	NEWSPAPER	An article about Marshall appears in the ___
33.	NICK	Dorothea married him.
34.	ORACLE	A place used to consult the deities
35.	OWL	One is named Thoth.
36.	PETEY	Elizabeth's parakeet they try to mummify
37.	PHARAOH	Marshall agreed to be one
38.	READING	Melanie's favorite past time
39.	ROSADA	Building where April and Melanie lived: Casa ___
40.	ROSS	Mr. ___ studies poetry and literature.
41.	SCHMITT	Owner of the variety store
42.	SECURITY	Marshall's octopus
43.	SET	Security was under his throne.
44.	SHED	Place where they found the bust of Nefertiti
45.	SINGER	Dorothea's occupation
46.	STAR	A shooting ___ was the secret omen on Halloween night.
47.	STONE	The Crocodile ___ rests on the altar of Set
48.	TEXTBOOK	April goes to Egypt with Marshall to get this
49.	THOTH	Serves as the oracle in the players' Egypt
50.	TOBY	Dressed as the New American
51.	WILSON	Name of the school

WORD SEARCH - The Egypt Game

```
R I S E T C E R E M O N Y G Y P S I E S
O I S D G N G E Y R C E K P L Y T H E H
S K M I T K S G B U T F O W E B A E H H
S N Z A S V I N R E C E O K H A R A L T
M E Q Y G R R I P A G R B B I S J D A S
U Z C M L I O S R L W T T M E T H Y S B
M D L U Q B N O B Q W I X R R E D G H N
M W P W R V L I G R P T E C O T A Q E C
I R F D Z I B L N D J I T H G S D I S R
F C G C N J T K I G D P P B L O A Y D P
I Z A E P S K Y D K D C W B Y R S D J A
C F E A T H E R A F N E K K P A Z H A T
A W H G K Y T K E P E C Q G H C P M E R
T I T F Y G N N R F I B P P I L T R E D
I L O X G P Y H L N N N R F C E H N I K
O S R H R T T J Y B O T E U S B O O K L
N O O V A V Q T V I T Q P W A T T S R E
T N D R N S I S S I H X K W S R H F I B
Y Z B F T N H U M K K Q G Y G P Y N H N
L I Q C G M L H O A R A H P X D A Z W N
L J Q I F L C Y T R V F M Q W L K P W R
X M D H A S N V R Z B D Q W E G F F E H
Q C W Y X L G M A R S H A M O S I S C R
```

AIDA	GYPSIES	PETEY
ALLUSION	HEAD	PHARAOH
APRIL	HIEROGLYPHICS	READING
BASTET	IMAGINING	ROSADA
BOOK	ISIS	ROSS
CAROLINE	KEN	SCHMITT
CEREMONY	KEYS	SECURITY
CURIO	LIBRARY	SET
DIGNITY	MARSHAMOSIS	SHED
DOROTHEA	MELANIE	SINGER
EGYPT	MUMMIFICATION	STAR
EYELASHES	NEFERTITI	STONE
FEATHER	NEWSPAPER	TEXTBOOK
FEBRUARY	NICK	THOTH
GIRL	ORACLE	TOBY
GRANT	OWL	WILSON

WORD SEARCH ANSWER KEY - The Egypt Game

```
R I S E T C E R E M O N Y G Y P S I E S
O I S           E       C E K   L Y T H E Y
S   M I         G       U T F O W E B A R E
S   A   S       R   N R E C   O K H A S D L
M E       G R I P A   R B   I   R A D   A
U   C     L I O   R     T X   E T   A   S
M   U       R   N       I T   R O T A     H
M     R       I G       T     G S   I     E
I       N       T   G         L O A D     S
F         A       Y   D       Y R S D     D
I         E                       P A   H A
C   F E A T H E R   A F N E K     H C P   E
A W H   G           E   E   C     I L T R D
T I     T Y         R   I   B     L E H N I
I L   O   G P Y       N     R     C   N   E
O S   R   R T       Y B O T E U   S B O O K L
N O   O   A N         T   I T   W   A T   E
  N   D   N T         S           R P H Y I
      B   G           U             P A N
L     I               M       H O A R A H P   E
    D A                               L P E
                  M A R S H A M O S I S     R
```

AIDA	GYPSIES	PETEY
ALLUSION	HEAD	PHARAOH
APRIL	HIEROGLYPHICS	READING
BASTET	IMAGINING	ROSADA
BOOK	ISIS	ROSS
CAROLINE	KEN	SCHMITT
CEREMONY	KEYS	SECURITY
CURIO	LIBRARY	SET
DIGNITY	MARSHAMOSIS	SHED
DOROTHEA	MELANIE	SINGER
EGYPT	MUMMIFICATION	STAR
EYELASHES	NEFERTITI	STONE
FEATHER	NEWSPAPER	TEXTBOOK
FEBRUARY	NICK	THOTH
GIRL	ORACLE	TOBY
GRANT	OWL	WILSON

CROSSWORD - The Egypt Game

Across

2. Melanie keeps her paper dolls in a geography ___.
4. A shooting ___ was the secret omen on Halloween night.
8. Elizabeth's parakeet they try to mummify
9. One is named Thoth.
10. Being a baby offended Marshall's
13. Kind of store the Professor owns
14. Melanie's Egyptian name
16. Policeman who investigates April's attack
18. The Summons from Set and ___
19. A shrunken one is brought for Set's altar.
21. The Professor gives these to the players
24. Serves as the oracle in the players' Egypt
25. Building where April and Melanie lived: Casa ___
26. Melanie's favorite past time
27. Dorothea married him.

Down

1. April's nickname
3. His Egyptian name is Horemheb.
4. Security was under his throne.
5. Mr. ___ studies poetry and literature.
6. An indirect reference to something
7. Identifies with the title character from Aida
10. Writes letters to April
11. A little ___ is murdered, bringing a halt to the Egypt Game.
12. Melanie's games with paper people
13. Dorothea's mother-in-law
15. Name of the gang's first pharaoh
17. Dressed as the New American
20. A place used to consult the deities
22. The Crocodile ___ rests on the altar of Set
23. Place where they found the bust of Nefertiti

CROSSWORD ANSWER KEY - The Egypt Game

		1 F	2 B	O	O	3 K		4 S	T	A	5 R		6 A
7 M |8 P	E	T	E	Y			E		E		9 O	W	L
E			B		10 D	I	11 G	N	12 I	T	Y		S		L
L		13 C	U	R	I	O		I		M			S		U
14 A	I	D	A		U	R		R		A		15 M			S
N			R		A			O		16 G	R	A	N	17 T	I
I			O		R			L		I		R		O	O
E			L		Y			H		N		S		B	N
	18 I	S	I	S		19 H	E	A	D		I		H		Y	
			N			A					N		A			20 O
	21 K	E	Y	S	22 S			23 S		G		M			R
					24 T	H	O	T	H		25 R	O	S	A	D	A
					O			E			S				C
26 R	E	A	D	I	N	G		D		27 N	I	C	K		L
					E						S				E

Across
2. Melanie keeps her paper dolls in a geography ___.
4. A shooting ___ was the secret omen on Halloween night.
8. Elizabeth's parakeet they try to mummify
9. One is named Thoth.
10. Being a baby offended Marshall's
13. Kind of store the Professor owns
14. Melanie's Egyptian name
16. Policeman who investigates April's attack
18. The Summons from Set and ___
19. A shrunken one is brought for Set's altar.
21. The Professor gives these to the players
24. Serves as the oracle in the players' Egypt
25. Building where April and Melanie lived: Casa ___
26. Melanie's favorite past time
27. Dorothea married him.

Down
1. April's nickname
3. His Egyptian name is Horemheb.
4. Security was under his throne.
5. Mr. ___ studies poetry and literature.
6. An indirect reference to something
7. Identifies with the title character from Aida
10. Writes letters to April
11. A little ___ is murdered, bringing a halt to the Egypt Game.
12. Melanie's games with paper people
13. Dorothea's mother-in-law
15. Name of the gang's first pharaoh
17. Dressed as the New American
20. A place used to consult the deities
22. The Crocodile ___ rests on the altar of Set
23. Place where they found the bust of Nefertiti

MATCHING 1 - The Egypt Game

___ 1. READING   A. Policeman who investigates April's attack
___ 2. HEAD   B. Dorothea's mother-in-law
___ 3. MELANIE   C. Melanie's Egyptian name
___ 4. HIEROGLYPHICS D. The ___ for the Dead
___ 5. GIRL   E. The Professor's real last name
___ 6. FEBRUARY   F. Melanie's games with paper people
___ 7. LIBRARY   G. Marshall's octopus
___ 8. CEREMONY   H. Name of the gang's first pharaoh
___ 9. HUDDLESTON   I. Preservation of dead bodies
___10. NEFERTITI   J. Egyptian writing system
___11. MUMMIFICATION K. Elizabeth reminded the girls of her
___12. AIDA   L. Identifies with the title character from Aida
___13. DOROTHEA   M. Writes letters to April
___14. PHARAOH   N. April's nickname
___15. ISIS   O. A little ___ is murdered, bringing a halt to the Egypt Game.
___16. KEN   P. Non-violent method of protest
___17. CURIO   Q. Kind of store the Professor owns
___18. CAROLINE   R. Serves as the oracle in the players' Egypt
___19. SECURITY   S. Marshall agreed to be one
___20. THOTH   T. Melanie's favorite past time
___21. DEMONSTRATION U. The Summons from Set and ___
___22. IMAGINING   V. Caroline's place of work
___23. GRANT   W. April claimed to want to be come an ___
___24. MARSHAMOSIS   X. His Egyptian name is Horemheb.
___25. ARCHAEOLOGIST Y. A shrunken one is brought for Set's altar.

MATCHING 1 ANSWER KEY - The Egypt Game

T - 1.	READING	A. Policeman who investigates April's attack
Y - 2.	HEAD	B. Dorothea's mother-in-law
L - 3.	MELANIE	C. Melanie's Egyptian name
J - 4.	HIEROGLYPHICS	D. The ___ for the Dead
O - 5.	GIRL	E. The Professor's real last name
N - 6.	FEBRUARY	F. Melanie's games with paper people
V - 7.	LIBRARY	G. Marshall's octopus
D - 8.	CEREMONY	H. Name of the gang's first pharaoh
E - 9.	HUDDLESTON	I. Preservation of dead bodies
K -10.	NEFERTITI	J. Egyptian writing system
I - 11.	MUMMIFICATION	K. Elizabeth reminded the girls of her
C -12.	AIDA	L. Identifies with the title character from Aida
M -13.	DOROTHEA	M. Writes letters to April
S -14.	PHARAOH	N. April's nickname
U -15.	ISIS	O. A little ___ is murdered, bringing a halt to the Egypt Game.
X -16.	KEN	P. Non-violent method of protest
Q -17.	CURIO	Q. Kind of store the Professor owns
B -18.	CAROLINE	R. Serves as the oracle in the players' Egypt
G -19.	SECURITY	S. Marshall agreed to be one
R -20.	THOTH	T. Melanie's favorite past time
P -21.	DEMONSTRATION	U. The Summons from Set and ___
F -22.	IMAGINING	V. Caroline's place of work
A -23.	GRANT	W. April claimed to want to be come an ___
H -24.	MARSHAMOSIS	X. His Egyptian name is Horemheb.
W 25.	ARCHAEOLOGIST	Y. A shrunken one is brought for Set's altar.

MATCHING 2 - The Egypt Game

___ 1. ISIS　　　　　　　　　　A. April goes to Egypt with Marshall to get this

___ 2. FEATHER　　　　　　　　B. Dorothea married him.

___ 3. PHARAOH　　　　　　　　C. The Summons from Set and ___

___ 4. LIBRARY　　　　　　　　D. Serves as the oracle in the players' Egypt

___ 5. GIRL　　　　　　　　　　E. One is named Thoth.

___ 6. SECURITY　　　　　　　　F. Name of the gang's first pharaoh

___ 7. ROSADA　　　　　　　　　G. The Professor gives these to the players

___ 8. ALLUSION　　　　　　　　H. Non-violent method of protest

___ 9. CEREMONY　　　　　　　　I. Kind of store the Professor owns

___ 10. THOTH　　　　　　　　　J. Marshall agreed to be one

___ 11. DIGNITY　　　　　　　　K. A little ___ is murdered, bringing a halt to the Egypt Game.

___ 12. DOROTHEA　　　　　　　L. It was the token Set and Isis sent as a summons.

___ 13. TEXTBOOK　　　　　　　M. The ___ for the Dead

___ 14. CAROLINE　　　　　　　N. Building where April and Melanie lived: Casa ___

___ 15. NICK　　　　　　　　　O. April's Egyptian name

___ 16. STAR　　　　　　　　　P. April claimed to want to be come an ___

___ 17. OWL　　　　　　　　　　Q. Preservation of dead bodies

___ 18. DEMONSTRATION　　　　R. Writes letters to April

___ 19. MUMMIFICATION　　　　S. Marshall's octopus

___ 20. KEYS　　　　　　　　　T. A shooting ___ was the secret omen on Halloween night.

___ 21. CURIO　　　　　　　　　U. Identifies with the title character from Aida

___ 22. ARCHAEOLOGIST　　　　V. Caroline's place of work

___ 23. MELANIE　　　　　　　W. Being a baby offended Marshall's

___ 24. BASTET　　　　　　　　X. Dorothea's mother-in-law

___ 25. MARSHAMOSIS　　　　　Y. An indirect reference to something

MATCHING 2 ANSWER KEY - The Egypt Game

C - 1. ISIS		A. April goes to Egypt with Marshall to get this
L - 2. FEATHER		B. Dorothea married him.
J - 3. PHARAOH		C. The Summons from Set and ___
V - 4. LIBRARY		D. Serves as the oracle in the players' Egypt
K - 5. GIRL		E. One is named Thoth.
S - 6. SECURITY		F. Name of the gang's first pharaoh
N - 7. ROSADA		G. The Professor gives these to the players
Y - 8. ALLUSION		H. Non-violent method of protest
M - 9. CEREMONY		I. Kind of store the Professor owns
D - 10. THOTH		J. Marshall agreed to be one
W - 11. DIGNITY		K. A little ___ is murdered, bringing a halt to the Egypt Game.
R - 12. DOROTHEA		L. It was the token Set and Isis sent as a summons.
A - 13. TEXTBOOK		M. The ___ for the Dead
X - 14. CAROLINE		N. Building where April and Melanie lived: Casa ___
B - 15. NICK		O. April's Egyptian name
T - 16. STAR		P. April claimed to want to be come an ___
E - 17. OWL		Q. Preservation of dead bodies
H - 18. DEMONSTRATION		R. Writes letters to April
Q - 19. MUMMIFICATION		S. Marshall's octopus
G - 20. KEYS		T. A shooting ___ was the secret omen on Halloween night.
I - 21. CURIO		U. Identifies with the title character from Aida
P - 22. ARCHAEOLOGIST		V. Caroline's place of work
U - 23. MELANIE		W. Being a baby offended Marshall's
O - 24. BASTET		X. Dorothea's mother-in-law
F - 25. MARSHAMOSIS		Y. An indirect reference to something

The Egypt Game Juggle Letter Review

1. EEINRTITF = 1. _____
Elizabeth reminded the girls of her

2. OSMSAIRMAHS = 2. _____
Name of the gang's first pharaoh

3. OADARS = 3. _____
Building where April and Melanie lived: Casa ___

4. IISS = 4. _____
The Summons from Set and ___

5. TOEDORAH = 5. _____
Writes letters to April

6. HFREEAT = 6. _____
It was the token Set and Isis sent as a summons.

7. NDIGYTI = 7. _____
Being a baby offended Marshall's

8. TYEEP = 8. _____
Elizabeth's parakeet they try to mummify

9. ALINMEE = 9. _____
Identifies with the title character from Aida

10. KOOETXTB =10. _____
April goes to Egypt with Marshall to get this

11. ESLAEHEYS =11. _____
Melanie stole April's

12. ANRTG =12. _____
Policeman who investigates April's attack

13. LNSULIOA =13. _____
An indirect reference to something

14. AEDH =14. _____
A shrunken one is brought for Set's altar.

15. ONTMNDSROIATE =15. _____
Non-violent method of protest

16. ESYK =16. _____
The Professor gives these to the players

17. OBYT =17. _____
Dressed as the New American

18. NYCMROEE =18. _____
The ___ for the Dead

19. IUTICANMMOMIF =19. _____
Preservation of dead bodies

20. ODTEUNDHLS =20. _____
The Professor's real last name

21. RLIARYB =21. _____
Caroline's place of work

22. RPWPEENAS =22. _____
An article about Marshall appears in the ___

23. HESD =23. _____
Place where they found the bust of Nefertiti

24. TTBEAS =24. _____
April's Egyptian name

25. ETS =25. _____
Security was under his throne.

26. TTHOH =26. _____
Serves as the oracle in the players' Egypt

27. YIHOGCREHLPSI =27. _____
Egyptian writing system

28. SIPGSEY =28. _____
Melanie, what do you know about ___?

29. TSIHCTM =29. _____
Owner of the variety store

30. LIACOREN =30. _____
Dorothea's mother-in-law

31. OSTNE =31. _____
The Crocodile ___ rests on the altar of Set

32. INMIINGGA =32. _____
Melanie's games with paper people

33. OKBO =33. _____
Melanie keeps her paper dolls in a geography ___.

34. LWO =34. _____
One is named Thoth.

35. ICROU =35. _____
Kind of store the Professor owns

36. SOSR =36. _____
Mr. ___ studies poetry and literature.

37. IRAPL =37. _____
She eventually gives up her false eyelashes.

38. NSLIOW =38. _____
Name of the school

39. CNIK =39. _____
Dorothea married him.

40. OAOLTRECHAGIS =40. _____
April claimed to want to be come an ___

41. ERCALO =41. _____
A place used to consult the deities

42. OAHHPRA =42. _____
Marshall agreed to be one

43. DAIA =43. _____
Melanie's Egyptian name

44. REUYSICT =44. _____
Marshall's octopus

45. TGYEP =45. _____
Place of fascination for April and Melanie

46. RNEGSI =46. _____
Dorothea's occupation

47. TRSA =47. _____
A shooting ___ was the secret omen on Halloween night.

The Egypt Game Juggle Letter Review Answer Key

1. EEINRTITF = 1. NEFERTITI
   Elizabeth reminded the girls of her

2. OSMSAIRMAHS = 2. MARSHAMOSIS
   Name of the gang's first pharaoh

3. OADARS = 3. ROSADA
   Building where April and Melanie lived: Casa ___

4. IISS = 4. ISIS
   The Summons from Set and ___

5. TOEDORAH = 5. DOROTHEA
   Writes letters to April

6. HFREEAT = 6. FEATHER
   It was the token Set and Isis sent as a summons.

7. NDIGYTI = 7. DIGNITY
   Being a baby offended Marshall's

8. TYEEP = 8. PETEY
   Elizabeth's parakeet they try to mummify

9. ALINMEE = 9. MELANIE
   Identifies with the title character from Aida

10. KOOETXTB =10. TEXTBOOK
    April goes to Egypt with Marshall to get this

11. ESLAEHEYS =11. EYELASHES
    Melanie stole April's

12. ANRTG =12. GRANT
    Policeman who investigates April's attack

13. LNSULIOA =13. ALLUSION
    An indirect reference to something

14. AEDH =14. HEAD
    A shrunken one is brought for Set's altar.

15. ONTMNDSROIATE =15. DEMONSTRATION
    Non-violent method of protest

16. ESYK =16. KEYS
The Professor gives these to the players

17. OBYT =17. TOBY
Dressed as the New American

18. NYCMROEE =18. CEREMONY
The ___ for the Dead

19. IUTICANMMOMIF =19. MUMMIFICATION
Preservation of dead bodies

20. ODTEUNDHLS =20. HUDDLESTON
The Professor's real last name

21. RLIARYB =21. LIBRARY
Caroline's place of work

22. RPWPEENAS =22. NEWSPAPER
An article about Marshall appears in the ___

23. HESD =23. SHED
Place where they found the bust of Nefertiti

24. TTBEAS =24. BASTET
April's Egyptian name

25. ETS =25. SET
Security was under his throne.

26. TTHOH =26. THOTH
Serves as the oracle in the players' Egypt

27. YIHOGCREHLPSI =27. HIEROGLYPHICS
Egyptian writing system

28. SIPGSEY =28. GYPSIES
Melanie, what do you know about ___?

29. TSIHCTM =29. SCHMITT
Owner of the variety store

30. LIACOREN =30. CAROLINE
Dorothea's mother-in-law

31. OSTNE =31. STONE
The Crocodile ___ rests on the altar of Set

32. INMIINGGA =32. IMAGINING
Melanie's games with paper people

33. OKBO =33. BOOK
Melanie keeps her paper dolls in a geography ___.

34. LWO =34. OWL
One is named Thoth.

35. ICROU =35. CURIO
Kind of store the Professor owns

36. SOSR =36. ROSS
Mr. ___ studies poetry and literature.

37. IRAPL =37. APRIL
She eventually gives up her false eyelashes.

38. NSLIOW =38. WILSON
Name of the school

39. CNIK =39. NICK
Dorothea married him.

40. OAOLTRECHAGIS =40. ARCHAEOLOGIST
April claimed to want to be come an ___

41. ERCALO =41. ORACLE
A place used to consult the deities

42. OAHHPRA =42. PHARAOH
Marshall agreed to be one

43. DAIA =43. AIDA
Melanie's Egyptian name

44. REUYSICT =44. SECURITY
Marshall's octopus

45. TGYEP =45. EGYPT
Place of fascination for April and Melanie

46. RNEGSI =46. SINGER
Dorothea's occupation

47. TRSA =47. STAR
A shooting ___ was the secret omen on Halloween night.

VOCABULARY RESOURCE MATERIALS

The Egypt Game Vocabulary Word List

No.	Word	Clue/Definition
1.	ABANDON	Absence of restraint
2.	ACCORD	Mutual agreement
3.	AMBITION	Strong desire to achieve something
4.	AMBUSHED	Hit with an unexpected attack
5.	ANTHROPOLOGY	Study of man, culture, and religion
6.	ASSOCIATE	Be around or spend time with
7.	BALEFULLY	Threateningly
8.	BIER	Portable platform on which a coffin is placed prior to burial
9.	BROODED	Worried over
10.	CASUALTIES	People hurt or killed in an incident
11.	CLAMORED	Demanded loudly
12.	COMMOTION	Noisy confusion
13.	CONSENSUS	General agreement
14.	CONSTERNATION	Anxiety; stress
15.	CONTEMPLATED	Considered; thought about intently
16.	CONVULSIONS	Fits of laughter
17.	CRINGED	Bent one's head and body in fear or embarrassment
18.	CURIOS	Rare or interesting objects
19.	DEFIANTLY	With open resistance
20.	DINGY	Grimy; shabby
21.	DISCLOSED	Revealed; told; showed
22.	DISPENSE	Do without
23.	DRASTIC	Extreme
24.	DRONE	Constant low humming sound
25.	ENTITLED	Had a right to
26.	ESCAPADES	Daring adventures
27.	EVASIVE	Cleverly avoiding
28.	EXALTED	Proud; glorified
29.	FALTERED	Wavered; hesitated
30.	FEROCIOUS	Fierce and cruel
31.	FIENDISH	Like a fiend; evil
32.	FLUENT	Able to write or speak easily
33.	FUMING	Showing a great deal of anger
34.	GINGERLY	Cautiously
35.	GLOAT	Smugly consider one's own success
36.	GRATIFYINGLY	In a pleasing manner
37.	GRUDGING	Reluctant or unwilling to give
38.	HAUGHTY	Arrogant
39.	IMPRESSION	A produced effect
40.	IMPROVISED	Created from whatever is available
41.	INCREDULOUS	Unbelieving
42.	INDIGNANT	Feeling irritated by treatment one feels is unfair
43.	INTEGRATE	Bring together into a whole
44.	LAIR	Hiding place
45.	LANGUISHING	Losing strength
46.	LEER	An evil, sidelong look
47.	LIABLE	Likely; apt
48.	MEDITATE	Focus the mind on spiritual matters for an uninterrupted period of time
49.	OBLIGED	Obligated; compelled by moral force

The Egypt Game Vocabulary Word List Continued

50. OCCUPATION — Way to spend time
51. OFFSET — Compensate for
52. OMEN — A sign that predicts a future event
53. ORACLE — Medium for divine prophecy
54. PERSISTENT — Enduring; continuing to exist; unrelenting
55. POMP — Showy display
56. PRIMITIVE — Relating to man's earliest existence
57. PRINCIPLES — Rules or beliefs that govern behavior
58. PROSPECT — Possibility or opportunity
59. PROSTRATION — Position of being stretched out on the ground
60. RELISH — Great enjoyment
61. RELUCTANT — Hesitant; not eager
62. RENDEZVOUS — Secret meeting
63. RESORT — To turn to out of necessity
64. REVENGE — Cause harm in response to harm done; get even
65. SCORNFULLY — With contempt
66. SCOUTED — Made a detailed search
67. SECLUSION — State of quiet separation from others
68. SELDOM — Not often
69. SHOWBOATING — Showing off
70. SIDLED — Moved sideways stealthily
71. SINISTER — Evil
72. SOLEMNITY — Formal, serious demeanor
73. SOPHISTICATE — Person who is cultured, fashionable, and refined
74. SPECULATED — Formed a theory without much evidence
75. SUMMONED — Called together
76. SUPERNATURAL — Unexplainable by the laws of nature
77. SWAGGER — Strut
78. SYMPATHETIC — Having an understanding or common feeling
79. TENDENCY — Inclination to behave a certain way
80. TORMENT — Annoy or tease severely
81. TREACHEROUS — Untrustworthy
82. UNISON — Together
83. VAPORS — Patches of rising moisture in the air
84. WARILY — Cautiously
85. WILT — Droop or weaken

VOCABULARY WORD SEARCH - The Egypt Game

```
A M B I T I O N S C O R N F U L L Y V B
G L O A T X C C J E A E S C A P A D E S
R E G G A W S O V D L S C E V I S A V E
C H T R D V V C N Z B D U M P V B M Z V
S W N U A Q T R O S E R O A C N F B C X
W Y E N R T Q Q S D E Z O M L Y G U U W
D K M I X H I B V E S N H O X T N S R M
H R R S Y R F F L S Q S S D L I H I B
D G O O G X X O Y T T O I U P E G E O M
Y L T N A I F E D I S C L O S E D D S S
P S I B E F L Q N T N Q E E M R U Z F X
R D F V S B B D Z N Z G R P M R S X P
I J Z E A P I D F E L P L Z Y N G N G C
N N T I B G E G R U T B Z Y L A I R S C
C L L W N G L C W E M D R V I E N T D M
I Y T A N W C B U W V I Q L R X T N Y S
P D N I L R A B A L J E N F A A E E C B
L T R L D E R E T L A F N G W L G U L H
E C G A S B O T E S E T H G F T R L A B
S W R V S D K D N C P F E A E E A F M F
C O L T R T E G D O O V U D D T R O K
S N M O R L I F E U M O B L I G E D R X
M J C E D I L C N T P W H X L I H V E W
L C B I N W D L C E J W J L B Y Q T D K
A C S R O P A V Y D M E D I T A T E Y Y
```

ACCORD	DRASTIC	INTEGRATE	SCORNFULLY
AMBITION	DRONE	LAIR	SCOUTED
AMBUSHED	ENTITLED	LEER	SELDOM
BALEFULLY	ESCAPADES	LIABLE	SIDLED
BIER	EVASIVE	MEDITATE	SOLEMNITY
BROODED	EXALTED	OBLIGED	SPECULATED
CASUALTIES	FALTERED	OFFSET	SWAGGER
CLAMORED	FLUENT	OMEN	TENDENCY
CONSENSUS	FUMING	ORACLE	TORMENT
CRINGED	GLOAT	POMP	UNISON
CURIOS	GRATIFYINGLY	PRINCIPLES	VAPORS
DEFIANTLY	GRUDGING	RELISH	WARILY
DINGY	HAUGHTY	RESORT	WILT
DISCLOSED	INDIGNANT	REVENGE	

VOCABULARY WORD SEARCH ANSWER KEY - The Egypt Game

ACCORD	DRASTIC	INTEGRATE	SCORNFULLY
AMBITION	DRONE	LAIR	SCOUTED
AMBUSHED	ENTITLED	LEER	SELDOM
BALEFULLY	ESCAPADES	LIABLE	SIDLED
BIER	EVASIVE	MEDITATE	SOLEMNITY
BROODED	EXALTED	OBLIGED	SPECULATED
CASUALTIES	FALTERED	OFFSET	SWAGGER
CLAMORED	FLUENT	OMEN	TENDENCY
CONSENSUS	FUMING	ORACLE	TORMENT
CRINGED	GLOAT	POMP	UNISON
CURIOS	GRATIFYINGLY	PRINCIPLES	VAPORS
DEFIANTLY	GRUDGING	RELISH	WARILY
DINGY	HAUGHTY	RESORT	WILT
DISCLOSED	INDIGNANT	REVENGE	

VOCABULARY CROSSWORD - The Egypt Game

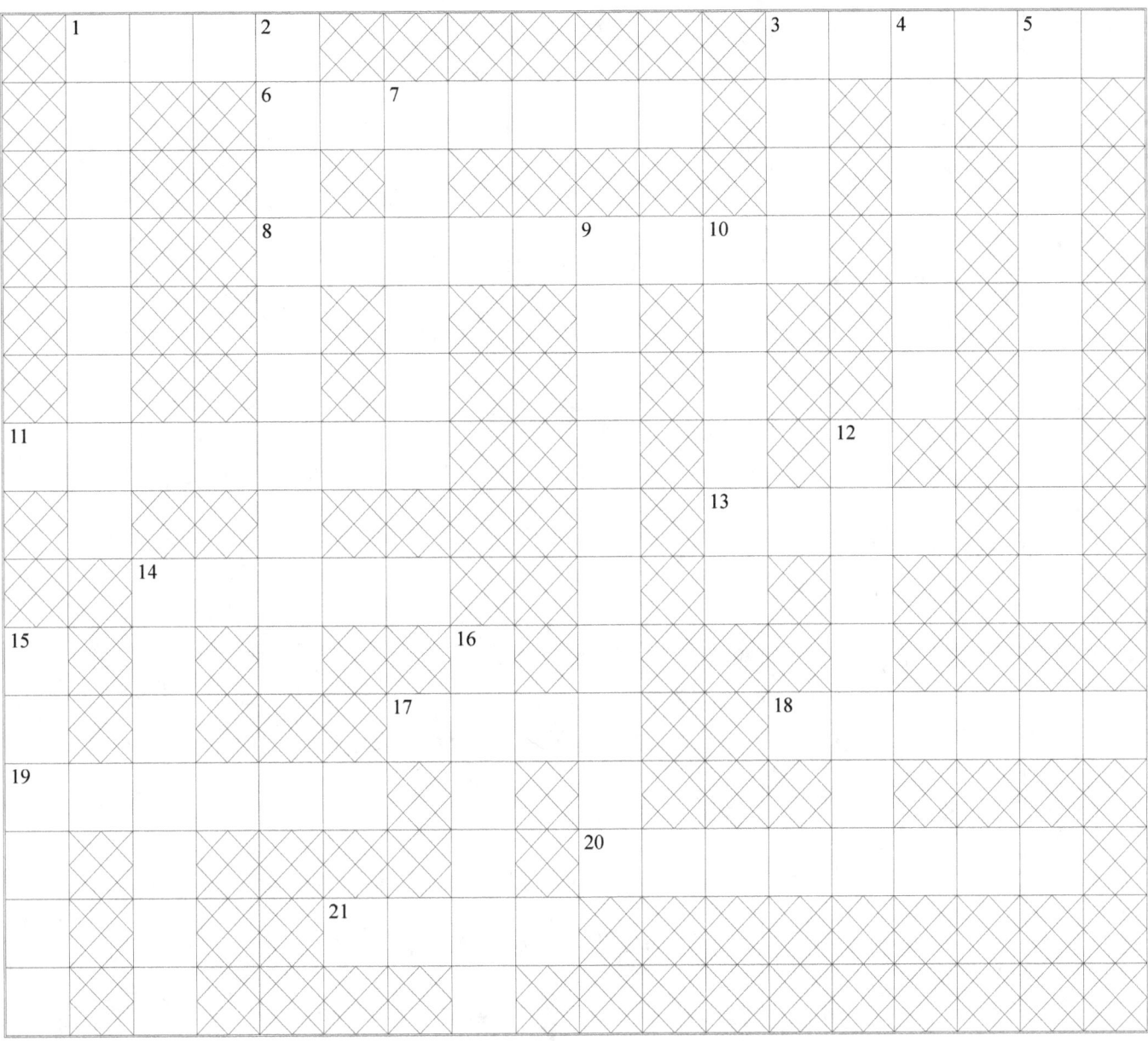

Across
1. Showy display
3. Compensate for
6. Proud; glorified
8. State of quiet separation from others
11. Made a detailed search
13. An evil, sidelong look
14. Grimy; shabby
17. Droop or weaken
18. Together
19. To turn to out of necessity
20. Do without
21. Portable platform on which a coffin is placed prior to burial

Down
1. Possibility or opportunity
2. Enduring; continuing to exist; unrelenting
3. A sign that predicts a future event
4. Showing a great deal of anger
5. Daring adventures
7. Mutual agreement
9. Formed a theory without much evidence
10. Medium for divine prophecy
12. Cause harm in response to harm done; get even
14. Extreme
15. Rare or interesting objects
16. Moved sideways stealthily

VOCABULARY CROSSWORD ANSWER KEY - The Egypt Game

	1 P	O	M	2 P						3 O	4 F	5 E	T
	R		6 E	X	7 A	L	T	E	D	M		U	S
	O		R		C					E		M	C
	S		8 S	E	C	L	U	9 S	10 I	O	N	I	A
	P		I		O			P	R			N	P
	E		S		R			E	A			G	A
11 S	C	O	U	T	E	D		C	C		12 R		D
	T		E					U	13 L	E	E	R	E
		14 D	I	N	G	Y		L	E		V		S
15 C		R		T		16 S	A				E		
U		A		17 W	I	L	T		18 U	N	I	S	O N
19 R	E	S	O	R	T				G				
I		T				20 D	I	S	P	E	N	S	E
O		I		21 B	I	E	R						
S		C				D							

Across
 1. Showy display
 3. Compensate for
 6. Proud; glorified
 8. State of quiet separation from others
11. Made a detailed search
13. An evil, sidelong look
14. Grimy; shabby
17. Droop or weaken
18. Together
19. To turn to out of necessity
20. Do without
21. Portable platform on which a coffin is placed prior to burial

Down
 1. Possibility or opportunity
 2. Enduring; continuing to exist; unrelenting
 3. A sign that predicts a future event
 4. Showing a great deal of anger
 5. Daring adventures
 7. Mutual agreement
 9. Formed a theory without much evidence
10. Medium for divine prophecy
12. Cause harm in response to harm done; get even
14. Extreme
15. Rare or interesting objects
16. Moved sideways stealthily

VOCABULARY MATCHING 1 - The Egypt Game

___ 1. FIENDISH   A. Evil
___ 2. GRATIFYINGLY   B. A sign that predicts a future event
___ 3. TORMENT   C. People hurt or killed in an incident
___ 4. SWAGGER   D. Bring together into a whole
___ 5. CASUALTIES   E. Like a fiend; evil
___ 6. SUMMONED   F. General agreement
___ 7. CONSENSUS   G. Bent one's head and body in fear or embarrassment
___ 8. BALEFULLY   H. Fierce and cruel
___ 9. INCREDULOUS   I. Great enjoyment
___ 10. ENTITLED   J. Strut
___ 11. SCORNFULLY   K. Called together
___ 12. ACCORD   L. Focus the mind on spiritual matters for an uninterrupted period of time
___ 13. OMEN   M. Compensate for
___ 14. RELISH   N. Annoy or tease severely
___ 15. EXALTED   O. Proud; glorified
___ 16. OFFSET   P. Unbelieving
___ 17. ABANDON   Q. Mutual agreement
___ 18. PROSPECT   R. Rules or beliefs that govern behavior
___ 19. INTEGRATE   S. Worried over
___ 20. PRINCIPLES   T. In a pleasing manner
___ 21. SINISTER   U. Possibility or opportunity
___ 22. CRINGED   V. Had a right to
___ 23. MEDITATE   W. Threateningly
___ 24. BROODED   X. Absence of restraint
___ 25. FEROCIOUS   Y. With contempt

VOCABULARY MATCHING 1 ANSWER KEY - The Egypt Game

E - 1. FIENDISH   A. Evil
T - 2. GRATIFYINGLY   B. A sign that predicts a future event
N - 3. TORMENT   C. People hurt or killed in an incident
J - 4. SWAGGER   D. Bring together into a whole
C - 5. CASUALTIES   E. Like a fiend; evil
K - 6. SUMMONED   F. General agreement
F - 7. CONSENSUS   G. Bent one's head and body in fear or embarrassment
W - 8. BALEFULLY   H. Fierce and cruel
P - 9. INCREDULOUS   I. Great enjoyment
V -10. ENTITLED   J. Strut
Y -11. SCORNFULLY   K. Called together
Q -12. ACCORD   L. Focus the mind on spiritual matters for an uninterrupted period of time
B -13. OMEN   M. Compensate for
I -14. RELISH   N. Annoy or tease severely
O -15. EXALTED   O. Proud; glorified
M -16. OFFSET   P. Unbelieving
X -17. ABANDON   Q. Mutual agreement
U -18. PROSPECT   R. Rules or beliefs that govern behavior
D -19. INTEGRATE   S. Worried over
R -20. PRINCIPLES   T. In a pleasing manner
A -21. SINISTER   U. Possibility or opportunity
G -22. CRINGED   V. Had a right to
L -23. MEDITATE   W. Threateningly
S -24. BROODED   X. Absence of restraint
H -25. FEROCIOUS   Y. With contempt

VOCABULARY MATCHING 2 - The Egypt Game

___ 1. BALEFULLY   A. Formal, serious demeanor
___ 2. DEFIANTLY   B. A sign that predicts a future event
___ 3. ANTHROPOLOGY   C. Extreme
___ 4. VAPORS   D. Reluctant or unwilling to give
___ 5. AMBITION   E. Moved sideways stealthily
___ 6. UNISON   F. Together
___ 7. SIDLED   G. Position of being stretched out on the ground
___ 8. FUMING   H. With open resistance
___ 9. ABANDON   I. Strong desire to achieve something
___10. LANGUISHING   J. Study of man, culture, and religion
___11. WILT   K. Enduring; continuing to exist; unrelenting
___12. RENDEZVOUS   L. Bring together into a whole
___13. GRUDGING   M. Droop or weaken
___14. PROSTRATION   N. Wavered; hesitated
___15. GRATIFYINGLY   O. Showing a great deal of anger
___16. CURIOS   P. Rare or interesting objects
___17. FALTERED   Q. In a pleasing manner
___18. RELUCTANT   R. Patches of rising moisture in the air
___19. OMEN   S. Secret meeting
___20. PERSISTENT   T. Losing strength
___21. GINGERLY   U. Arrogant
___22. HAUGHTY   V. Cautiously
___23. INTEGRATE   W. Absence of restraint
___24. SOLEMNITY   X. Hesitant; not eager
___25. DRASTIC   Y. Threateningly

VOCABULARY MATCHING 2 ANSWER KEY - The Egypt Game

Y - 1. BALEFULLY   A. Formal, serious demeanor
H - 2. DEFIANTLY   B. A sign that predicts a future event
J - 3. ANTHROPOLOGY   C. Extreme
R - 4. VAPORS   D. Reluctant or unwilling to give
I - 5. AMBITION   E. Moved sideways stealthily
F - 6. UNISON   F. Together
E - 7. SIDLED   G. Position of being stretched out on the ground
O - 8. FUMING   H. With open resistance
W   9. ABANDON   I. Strong desire to achieve something
T -10. LANGUISHING   J. Study of man, culture, and religion
M 11. WILT   K. Enduring; continuing to exist; unrelenting
S -12. RENDEZVOUS   L. Bring together into a whole
D -13. GRUDGING   M. Droop or weaken
G -14. PROSTRATION   N. Wavered; hesitated
Q -15. GRATIFYINGLY   O. Showing a great deal of anger
P -16. CURIOS   P. Rare or interesting objects
N -17. FALTERED   Q. In a pleasing manner
X -18. RELUCTANT   R. Patches of rising moisture in the air
B -19. OMEN   S. Secret meeting
K -20. PERSISTENT   T. Losing strength
V -21. GINGERLY   U. Arrogant
U -22. HAUGHTY   V. Cautiously
L -23. INTEGRATE   W. Absence of restraint
A -24. SOLEMNITY   X. Hesitant; not eager
C -25. DRASTIC   Y. Threateningly

The Egypt Game Vocabulary Juggle Review 1

1. RAOPOLGYTHNO = 1. _____
   Study of man, culture, and religion

2. EESIAVV = 2. _____
   Cleverly avoiding

3. MCELDROA = 3. _____
   Demanded loudly

4. SCIUOR = 4. _____
   Rare or interesting objects

5. DCENRGI = 5. _____
   Bent one's head and body in fear or embarrassment

6. DINGY = 6. _____
   Grimy; shabby

7. IELNDAFYT = 7. _____
   With open resistance

8. DEPOALMNCTTE = 8. _____
   Considered; through about intently

9. ATUGHYH = 9. _____
   Arrogant

10. UNELCIDOUSR =10. _____
    Unbelieving

11. XLEDTAE =11. _____
    Proud; glorified

12. CPEDASSAE =12. _____
    Daring adventures

13. NOANBAD =13. _____
    Absence of restraint

14. OIMTOMNCO =14. _____
    Noisy confusion

15. LYLEAUBLF =15. _____
    Threateningly

16. GNERIYGL =16. _____
   Cautiously

17. BTIMAION =17. _____
   Strong desire to achieve something

18. NVOCUSOSLIN =18. _____
   Fits of laughter

19. OCITETNNSNRAO =19. _____
   Anxiety; stress

20. GRUINDGG =20. _____
   Reluctant or unwilling to give

21. SORFOIUCE =21. _____
   Fierce and cruel

22. OCRDCA =22. _____
   Mutual agreement

23. RIPOEMSIVD =23. _____
   Created from whatever is available

24. ESDPSNIE =24. _____
   Do without

25. IREB =25. _____
   Portable platform on which a coffin is placed prior to burial

26. ISATECALUS =26. _____
   People hurt or killed in an incident

27. NRESOIPMIS =27. _____
   A produced effect

28. NRODE =28. _____
   Constant low humming sound

29. LDDEISSOC =29. _____
   Revealed; told; showed

30. IISDEFHN =30. _____
   Like a fiend; evil

31. YGGIANRFLTIY =31. _____
   In a pleasing manner

32. MNGFIU =32. _____
Showing a great deal of anger

33. SSECNUOSN =33. _____
General agreement

34. NFUTEL =34. _____
Able to write or speak easily

35. RFLEADET =35. _____
Wavered; hesitated

36. COSASITAE =36. _____
Be around or spend time with

37. OATGL =37. _____
Smugly consider one's own success

38. ESDMUHAB =38. _____
Hit with an unexpected attack

The Egypt Game Vocabulary Juggle Letter 1 Review Answer Key

1. RAOPOLGYTHNO = 1. ANTHROPOLOGY
   Study of man, culture, and religion

2. EESIAVV = 2. EVASIVE
   Cleverly avoiding

3. MCELDROA = 3. CLAMORED
   Demanded loudly

4. SCIUOR = 4. CURIOS
   Rare or interesting objects

5. DCENRGI = 5. CRINGED
   Bent one's head and body in fear or embarrassment

6. DINGY = 6. DINGY
   Grimy; shabby

7. IELNDAFYT = 7. DEFIANTLY
   With open resistance

8. DEPOALMNCTTE = 8. CONTEMPLATED
   Considered; through about intently

9. ATUGHYH = 9. HAUGHTY
   Arrogant

10. UNELCIDOUSR = 10. INCREDULOUS
    Unbelieving

11. XLEDTAE = 11. EXALTED
    Proud; glorified

12. CPEDASSAE = 12. ESCAPADES
    Daring adventures

13. NOANBAD = 13. ABANDON
    Absence of restraint

14. OIMTOMNCO = 14. COMMOTION
    Noisy confusion

15. LYLEAUBLF = 15. BALEFULLY
    Threateningly

16. GNERIYGL =16. GINGERLY
Cautiously

17. BTIMAION =17. AMBITION
Strong desire to achieve something

18. NVOCUSOSLIN =18. CONVULSIONS
Fits of laughter

19. OCITETNNSNRAO =19. CONSTERNATION
Anxiety; stress

20. GRUINDGG =20. GRUDGING
Reluctant or unwilling to give

21. SORFOIUCE =21. FEROCIOUS
Fierce and cruel

22. OCRDCA =22. ACCORD
Mutual agreement

23. RIPOEMSIVD =23. IMPROVISED
Created from whatever is available

24. ESDPSNIE =24. DISPENSE
Do without

25. IREB =25. BIER
Portable platform on which a coffin is placed prior to burial

26. ISATECALUS =26. CASUALTIES
People hurt or killed in an incident

27. NRESOIPMIS =27. IMPRESSION
A produced effect

28. NRODE =28. DRONE
Constant low humming sound

29. LDDEISSOC =29. DISCLOSED
Revealed; told; showed

30. IISDEFHN =30. FIENDISH
Like a fiend; evil

31. YGGIANRFLTIY =31. GRATIFYINGLY
In a pleasing manner

32. MNGFIU =32. FUMING
Showing a great deal of anger

33. SSECNUOSN =33. CONSENSUS
General agreement

34. NFUTEL =34. FLUENT
Able to write or speak easily

35. RFLEADET =35. FALTERED
Wavered; hesitated

36. COSASITAE =36. ASSOCIATE
Be around or spend time with

37. OATGL =37. GLOAT
Smugly consider one's own success

38. ESDMUHAB =38. AMBUSHED
Hit with an unexpected attack

Egypt Game Vocabulary Juggle Letter Review 2

1. IWLT = 1. _____
   Droop or weaken

2. OEERZUVNSD = 2. _____
   Secret meeting

3. OUSCDTE = 3. _____
   Made a detailed search

4. ERTROS = 4. _____
   To turn to out of necessity

5. AITMDEET = 5. _____
   Focus the mind on spiritual matters for an uninterrupted period of time

6. EGNEVER = 6. _____
   Cause harm in response to harm done; get even

7. RTEOTMN = 7. _____
   Annoy or tease severely

8. PIITACEOSTHS = 8. _____
   Person who is cultured, fashionable, and refined

9. RLEE = 9. _____
   An evil, sidelong look

10. IUSONN = 10. _____
    Together

11. OVPRSA = 11. _____
    Patches of rising moisture in the air

12. OCENSISLU = 12. _____
    State of quiet separation from others

13. EMON = 13. _____
    A sign that predicts a future event

14. IVITIEMRP = 14. _____
    Relating to man's earliest existence

15. LLCUOSFNRY = 15. _____
    With contempt

16. PPMO = 16. _____
Showy display

17. RIAL = 17. _____
Hiding place

18. ETIINSSR = 18. _____
Evil

19. UNSIINGALHG = 19. _____
Losing strength

20. OSNIABGHTOW = 20. _____
Showing off

21. NTIDNGNAI = 21. _____
Feeling irritated by treatment one feels is unfair

22. TNARROPSOTI = 22. _____
Position of being stretched out on the ground

23. LECDTEAPSU = 23. _____
Formed a theory without much evidence

24. RIWAYL = 24. _____
Cautiously

25. EDDILS = 25. _____
Moved sideways stealthily

26. LOESDM = 26. _____
Not often

27. LAPAUNUSTRER = 27. _____
Unexplainable by the laws of nature

28. EOGBILD = 28. _____
Obligated; compelled by moral force

29. AYETHMPSICT = 29. _____
Having an understanding or common feeling

30. TPSOPERC = 30. _____
Possibility or opportunity

31. IPRNTSEETS = 31. _____
Enduring; continuing to exist; unrelenting

32. ESHLRI = 32. _____
Great enjoyment

33. RSGWGEA =33. _____
Strut

34. NYELOITSM =34. _____
Formal, serious demeanor

35. LIBAEL =35. _____
Likely; apt

36. SFEOTF =36. _____
Compensate for

37. ARLCOE =37. _____
Medium for divine prophecy

38. TTAGEIERN =38. _____
Bring together into a whole

39. MDMEOUSN =39. _____
Called together

40. CELNPSRIPI =40. _____
Rules or beliefs that govern behavior

41. RTCUEOARHSE =41. _____
Untrustworthy

42. CUCITNOOAP =42. _____
Way to spend time

43. ENCEYNTD =43. _____
Inclination to behave a certain way

Egypt Game Vocabulary Juggle Letter Review 2 Answer Key

1. IWLT = 1. WILT
Droop or weaken

2. OEERZUVNSD = 2. RENDEZVOUS
Secret meeting

3. OUSCDTE = 3. SCOUTED
Made a detailed search

4. ERTROS = 4. RESORT
To turn to out of necessity

5. AITMDEET = 5. MEDITATE
Focus the mind on spiritual matters for an uninterrupted period of time

6. EGNEVER = 6. REVENGE
Cause harm in response to harm done; get even

7. RTEOTMN = 7. TORMENT
Annoy or tease severely

8. PIITACEOSTHS = 8. SOPHISTICATE
Person who is cultured, fashionable, and refined

9. RLEE = 9. LEER
An evil, sidelong look

10. IUSONN = 10. UNISON
Together

11. OVPRSA = 11. VAPORS
Patches of rising moisture in the air

12. OCENSISLU = 12. SECLUSION
State of quiet separation from others

13. EMON = 13. OMEN
A sign that predicts a future event

14. IVITIEMRP = 14. PRIMITIVE
Relating to man's earliest existence

15. LLCUOSFNRY = 15. SCORNFULLY
With contempt

16. PPMO = 16. POMP
Showy display

17. RIAL = 17. LAIR
Hiding place

18. ETIINSSR = 18. SINISTER
Evil

19. UNSIINGALHG = 19. LANGUISHING
Losing strength

20. OSNIABGHTOW = 20. SHOWBOATING
Showing off

21. NTIDNGNAI = 21. INDIGNANT
Feeling irritated by treatment one feels is unfair

22. TNARROPSOTI = 22. PROSTRATION
Position of being stretched out on the ground

23. LECDTEAPSU = 23. SPECULATED
Formed a theory without much evidence

24. RIWAYL = 24. WARILY
Cautiously

25. EDDILS = 25. SIDLED
Moved sideways stealthily

26. LOESDM = 26. SELDOM
Not often

27. LAPAUNUSTRER = 27. SUPERNATURAL
Unexplainable by the laws of nature

28. EOGBILD = 28. OBLIGED
Obligated; compelled by moral force

29. AYETHMPSICT = 29. SYMPATHETIC
Having an understanding or common feeling

30. TPSOPERC = 30. PROSPECT
Possibility or opportunity

31. IPRNTSEETS = 31. PERSISTENT
Enduring; continuing to exist; unrelenting

32. ESHLRI = 32. RELISH
Great enjoyment

33. RSGWGEA =33. SWAGGER
Strut

34. NYELOITSM =34. SOLEMNITY
Formal, serious demeanor

35. LIBAEL =35. LIABLE
Likely; apt

36. SFEOTF =36. OFFSET
Compensate for

37. ARLCOE =37. ORACLE
Medium for divine prophecy

38. TTAGEIERN =38. INTEGRATE
Bring together into a whole

39. MDMEOUSN =39. SUMMONED
Called together

40. CELNPSRIPI =40. PRINCIPLES
Rules or beliefs that govern behavior

41. RTCUEOARHSE =41. TREACHEROUS
Untrustworthy

42. CUCITNOOAP =42. OCCUPATION
Way to spend time

43. ENCEYNTD =43. TENDENCY
Inclination to behave a certain way

www.ingramcontent.com/pod-product-compliance
Lightning Source LLC
Chambersburg PA
CBHW051405070526
44584CB00023B/3300